PANDEMIC POETRY
AND REFLECTIONS

Carolina Ayala-Velasquez

DEDICATION

This book is dedicated to everyone searching for themselves. This journey of life is a constant learning experience. Pandemic or not, life has its challenges. I truly believe that everything happens for a reason(s), even when I do not understand what that reason may be.

This book will not be my everyday diary (but it may feel that way.) It will be some shared reflections, and poetry that I put together. It will not be perfect; it will have errors and it will be "unpolished." It will be real, honest and I will be proud.

This book is to show myself and others that you can get anything done. You can create more; you can make changes later. What matters to me right now, is getting this out there-for whatever it becomes. Whatever it will be, that is what matters to me.

As a writer, I will always have more to say. I will always have more I wish I wrote. I will always want to add or take out. This books completion isn't about that. It's about getting it done.

A message to my reader: I am not sure when the day will come that I will care too much about typo's and perfection. Right now, I believe my message is to do what I love, create what makes me happy and share it with the world, as is. Right now, I want to show others you can write your books and they do not need to be perfect. You can follow your dreams without perfectionism, and you can still make a difference.

I wrote this book, for me. I wanted to pull together my story and my journey. I wanted to have a living book, that will live beyond me. I want to touch lives.

This is dedicated to the writers, the dreamers, the perfectionists, the do-ers, those struggling and those moving forward. This is to anyone who finds their way to read a single word. This is for anyone who manages to come across the pages. This is for you, whatever brought you here-I don't believe in coincidence, you were meant to be right here-right now.

I thank you.

CAROLINA AYALA-VELASQUEZ

CONTENTS

INTRODUCTION

Pandemic
[panˈdemik]
NOUN

> a widespread occurrence of an
> infectious disease over a whole country
> or the world at a particular time.
> "the impact of the pandemic caused
> loved ones to be separated and unable
> to meet in person"

The years before the pandemic, my life was already drastically changing. More specifically, January 11, 2019, my dream job closed. It was a job in which I found my career. It was a place where I had been at for so much of my life and yet barley started at its new location. It all came full circle, a story for another time... Or what better time than now?

I always knew from a very young age that I wanted to grow up and become a teacher. In high-school I knew more than ever that was my calling. After I graduated high-school I became a mom and attended community college until graduating with my AA degree in child development in 2012. I was so excited to be able to go back to my former high school to teach in the pre-school. I spent the next 7 years teaching, 3 different locations. These three locations were all connected because of Alternatives in Action (AIA,) the families served and my dream.

In January 2019 not only did my journey at Alternatives In Action Preschool come to an end, but my family was also told we needed to move in the next few months. I had lived in this home for more than half of my life, the same timeframe of my involvement with AIA (teaching.)

I spent the year of 2019 accepting reality, moving along with the moving pieces, grieving and healing. I spent this time participating in free coaching opportunities, learning about scholarships, I started counseling, and became more in alignment with myself. Not rushing to work just any job, really wanting one that I love. Really allowing myself the time and space to feel all I was feeling from the big transitions. Time to sit with it, time to start healing and then knowing eventually I will find my way into what's meant for me.

We did home-school for the first half of the 2019 school year. Which had been on our mind and hearts for years.

2020 was all about continuing my self-care and healing journey. I have known self-care all my life, gratitude saved me. Self-care to me has always been writing, reflecting, practicing gratitude, helping others, creating poetry, taking photos, making meaningful gifts for others, listening to music, and sharing my story.

Self-care also used to look like indulging in shopping, indulging in eating and mindless scrolling.

These days my self-care is evolving into spending money on investing in myself: in coaching groups, in making my dreams reality. It means being more intentional with all the layers of me and not just taking in information but applying it. This year is all about trying new things and hopefully getting new results. What is not working, isn't working. Everything has served me, and I am being called to do different. To trust in the unknown. "Faith over Fear" was my 2020 mantra and finding my Zen. I wanted peace.

The pandemic wasn't all "worst time ever" or "dream come true." 2020 wasn't all about wealth and all good things. I have struggles, challenges, fear, hardships. I found myself feeling jealousy and victimhood when others were getting unemployment or stimulus checks and my family wasn't. Our family was at the food banks, my husband the only one working and his hours were cut and changed due to the pandemic. We signed up for toy drives for the holidays, reached out to support groups.

When our household got c19, we all had different symptoms. My husband was out of work for quarantine, and- he was the only one working. People brought us groceries and things because we couldn't go out. C19 meant special days without those we loved. My husband's mom has cancer and the fear of the virus made everything unsure. We were scared to see our family or sleep with our children. I questioned the path I was on of holisticness, self-care and trusting my inner guidance.

But despite all of that, the true pandemics first year was also a lot of peace, dream come true and embracing the good. The first two weeks of shelter in place we embraced being home just us. When my husband was called essential, we felt like it meant he was super important while also disposable. I knew I needed my kids in fresh air, without masks-getting exercise-while following guidelines. The thoughts and fears came, about losing more time with our oldest child whom we share between homes. However, instead, we fought and pushed for the life we have always hoped for. To have 50/50 time with him. Because of the pandemic, the rules, the fears and making the most of hard times- we started sharing time between homes by having him every other week. I knew the following year (2021) would be more about direction and this year would be the trial year that allowed grace through error-so I ran with it all. I embraced this year of 2020 that so many were fearing. We took trips, we stayed home, we stayed to us, we faced c19 and sickness and the forever changing rules and regulations.

The more I listened to my heart, leaned into resources, lived in my truth-the more everything started coming to us. The money came in-in different ways. Right away, when money would come- I debated what I would do. Then I said no, I have to do everything I said I would do if we were given the money to do so. I kept leaning into faith and alignment and the more I did, the more that came. Help and abundance showed up in all forms, constantly.

I do believe you will hear the same messages over and over, in different ways- until you answer and step into what you are being called to do. I was finally hearing and seeing and accepting these messages. I was finally ready to hear and see differently.

Not everything always worked out. But it did.

So much did work out. I invested in people I believe in. I invested in me. I invested in whatever felt like it was in alignment. I started caring about my skin and my health in new ways. Things I never really cared about, I started paying attention to.

I am not a doctor, and I am not an expert at anything. I am just a person. I am just someone telling my story and sharing my journey. What I am sharing is not to push you in any way that my way is the right way or that your way is somehow wrong. I am a life-long learner, and I am forever growing and evolving and changing. We are all going through this journey of life without a manual and we will all have different stories, learnings, and teachings. I am simply sharing my pandemic journey because I feel called to share it, because I want to remember it. Maybe some will relate, I know some wont. But I feel like we can all learn from each other, support each other, help each other realize new things, think new thoughts---all in which help each of us live into and find our life purpose even more.

This pandemic I feel like is testing everything for me. Testing my faith in all I want to believe and do believe. (Doctors, money, herbalism, homeschool, co-parenting, addictions, self-care.)

2021 is all about staying in my truth. Staying true to who I am. Continuing to align with me, with my purpose, my callings and continue finding myself through listening to my inner voices. I committed to applying what I have learned to be true-especially in the moments of doubt and fear.

What message have you heard over and over, that is waiting to be embraced?

_____

_____

_____

_____

_____

_____

_____

_____

_____

What am I scared of?

Why do I fear success?

What will it mean to put me first? To go after my dreams. To prioritize me?

How many times have you ever said to yourself?

If I had the time, I would_____.

If I had the money, I would_____.

If I had the resources, I would_____.

If I had the time, money and knew the steps (I would finally write that book.)

If I had the privilege to homeschool, I would.

If I had the time to put me first, I would.

If I had extra time, I would finally workout.

If I had the money: I would get matching furniture, get coaching, put my health first, buy organic, get massages, see a chiropractor and take trips.

How many times have you thought and believed...?

Why does the bad always happen to me?

I can never get ahead because I'm always behind.

Being broke is what's holding me back. Even with full time work, I have no money to invest in my dreams. It's hard enough to just survive.

What if you could believe and know, that abundance is all around? What if you could be grateful daily for everything happening to and for you?

What if, the pandemic is just another situation we must get through?

Life has always been filled with challenge and hardship. Can you embrace the goodness that is?

Truth is, time doesn't change. Even when in different time zones. We all have the same amount of time to work with. We all have priorities. We all have different privileges, talents, gifts, and mindsets.

For me, this pandemic and time in my life was about learning to trust. I can't say I always trust others and myself, but I am leaning into faith more. I had finally reached the point of wanting to try new things, whether I believed they would be that life changing factor or not. I had to let go of old stories and work on me every day. I had to start loving me the way I love others.

I started taking advantage of opportunities such as scholarships. I started building a new relationship with money, time, and myself.

As I started to step into what was in alignment with my heart more, with my dreams and things started falling into place more and more.

As I started to put me first, I started to realize and learn-I wasn't putting my family last or second. Loving me and taking care of me, meant I could be better for them and teach them how to love on themselves too. I started realizing this wasn't just for them or for me, it was for all of us.

It wasn't easy. Change is never easy, at least not for me. It takes thought work, mindset shifts, prayer, support and knowing your "why,"

Lately, I am changing my relationship with money. I want it to feel better: making it, spending it, having it. So, I am looking at my money flow, what comes in and out. Being more intentional with how I use it. I am paying more attention to even how I store it in my wallet.

The way this book is written is in no particular order of how life unfolded for me during this pandemic time. So much happened simultaneously. This book is a compilation of many journals and social media posts, combined into one book. It is not everything and it doesn't end with the last page of this particular book. The dates are for me and my documentation, but there's no need to try to piece them together.

If you take anything from this, whether you feel similar or not- I hope you find things to think about, I hope it helps you reflect and I hope you get inspired.

What are you afraid of? Don't hold back. Let it out.

_____

_____

_____

_____

_____

_____

_____

_____

_____

TINY BOOK

I had been googling for a while "how to write a book." "How to become an author."

Everything was so expensive; I could never afford any of it. I wrote pages of notes, wish lists and more. Others were living their dreams; I knew it was possible but yet I didn't know how to make it real.

I had been talking with my coach Julie Neale for many years. She knew my dream of wanting to write books. It wasn't until more recent years where the whispers became louder screams in my heart saying this is where it wanted me to go-that the opportunity of the tiny book course would come up.

August 17, 2020, after a coaching call with Julie, she shared a link to the tiny book course with Alexandra Franzen and Lindsey smith. She encouraged me to ask if they had scholarships available. Asking for a scholarship was very hard for me. I felt like a charity case, I was scared of rejection and judgement. I was also inspired by my heart-I knew now was the time and I had to try or else I would regret not knowing. I told myself 'If I get this scholarship then it's meant to be." I heard back pretty quickly- that no scholarships were available. They offered several payment options, the classic option being the cheapest and with early bird pricing it would be $595.

That's basically $600 dollars and I am out of work. My husband is working his butt off with less hours and everything constantly changing and uncertain in this pandemic. We hadn't gotten any stimulus checks or unemployment or anything at this point. I thought of all the things "what's the catch, does this cost really cover everything? I am sure it will cost more, and do I have that to invest and gamble with?"

What will it mean to do this? Will it mean I am taking away from my family and making life harder for us? Will me investing in this be all for nothing if I don't succeed?

"If I use my bill money, will I make it back in time to take care of what I need it for?"

Julie was thinking of taking the course as well. She even had an idea of anyone from Mothers Quest who joined, that we could have check in circles outside of the tiny book course-as extra support. Also, that mothersquest was an affiliate. Mothersquest is a podcast and community and space that has meant a lot to me over the last five years. I was now motivated by wanting to support mothers' quest and to do this in community with people I admire. I wanted to take risk, get the early bird pricing and I wanted to do this for me. The course would start in October, my birthday month- and I thought "what a perfect gift to give myself, the gift of finally becoming an author." I knew I didn't want to be on the sidelines months from now only celebrating others who would get it done, I wanted to be amongst those who would be celebrated.

August 28, 2020 -I signed up and paid. I felt relief that I no longer had to decide or go back and forth. I felt scared still, how would I now get the money I used that we need for rent and bills and life.

I was hoping for money and trusting it would come but still not feeling too sure.

Once I made that investment and commitment and leap of faith, everything else started falling in place.

The course was from Oct1-Nov 15. Although the course had finished up in November, I was still motivated to get it done. I was too close not to. It could be too easy to not finish and then go down that road of "I wish" and regret. So, I kept working. Motivated to be in the upcoming tiny book course photoshoot.

I uploaded and published my book On Dec 7 and by Dec 29 my books finally arrived and were in my hands.

"Healing while Hurting, poetry and reflections" went on sale on Amazon on my dad's 7-year anniversary of his passing January 21, 2021.

I was able to be a part of the tiny book course first ever virtual book fair this year of 2021.

In 2021 I came across the thought again. Do I want to join again? I thought I would have my next book done early in 2021, because I know knew what to expect and how to get it done. I still hadn't had it done and it was halfway through the year. Once again, I didn't have the money to invest or gamble with. I knew I didn't "need" to do

19

it. However, the course was taking place and would end on my birthday this year. People I care about were taking the course. No scholarships were available. I was offered a discount for being a returning member. I was able to become an affiliate and possibly earn commissions.

I joined again. I wanted to get this done, I wanted support, I wanted to be in community. Investing money lights a fire under your butt to accomplish the task.

I knew after last year, that I wanted to write a poetry book based on writings from the span of my life-time. When I started putting it together this year, I decided I wasn't ready to dig that deep, re-live that past and offer it to the world yet. I then changed my mind and decided to put together a book I had already created on paper with my children for my mom. This made more sense to complete because it is the reason, I joined the tiny book course in the first place but decided on something different. I want to create a children's book, about my mom. My children helped create the pictures. We decided it would be good enough because what mattered was that it finally got done, for her. I also wanted to win my tuition back, whoever was first to get their book in their hands would win this. I did not win; I literally was off by a couple of hours. But I got it done. My mom and family love it.

This book was completed in time for graduation and although it is personal and just for our family- I am beyond proud. I plan to one day have the illustrator of my dreams and create this book in the way I vision to be sold in book stores.

When I completed this book, I still wanted a book to go on sale. The idea of "Pandemic Poetry, and reflections" came to me. I thought I could get it done by the end date of October 15, but as I sit here still putting it together and it is December 15- it is clear, I needed more time.

I am not giving up, once again motivated to be in the photoshoot and to have another book go on sale for this upcoming new year. It will get done.

Lena Ayala-Velasquez
November 12, 2020 ·
Shared with Your friends

You may feel behind, unaccomplished, lost, stuck, scared....

you may feel so many things. and it is ok.

I encourage you to share your truth and journey. Someone out there often feels the same, someone out there might have needed to hear what you had to say.

by sharing, you create release, relief and growth. You create courage, hope and trust.

I have been feeling a whirlwind of emotions while writing this book.

Someone today asked me about it. Asked me how I was doing it. She said she had always wanted to write a book and asked if I could share the link of the course, I am going through.

she told me "So many people often think, I want to write a book, and they don't do it-you are doing it! you did it!"

whether someone hits like, love or leaves a comment- people are watching and reading what you share.

You never know who you are inspiring.

you never know the connections you are making when you are open.

As I was writing this post, I then came across this next part, and it all ties in so well......

*Julie Neale of MothersQuest posted this:

What are some of YOUR favorite things? What work in your world is lighting you up? What collaborations are giving you fuel to keep doing what you do? Would love to hear ✨✨✨ and I love questions like this and time to reflect and dig a little deeper.

Some of my favorite things are being with my family. Embracing being home with the kids, although I am not "working" I am enjoying being home and helping with school. I love writing, taking photos and creating special gifts for people. So much work in the world is lighting me up: I am so thankful for the teachers(I am thankful to have been one, to be one- even if I am technically not being paid for it right now), I am thankful for the investment in chiropractic help-all I am learning and feeling and how it is helping change me for the better, I am so thankful for all of the coaches in my life and for me being able to help others, although I do not yet call myself a "coach". The fuel to keep going and doing what I do is gratitude. Every day I have so much gratitude for all that's in my life. Right now, I am so thankful to be a part of mother's quest and the tiny book course, I am so thankful to be in soul care with barb Klein and the courageous life society with

Jessica Stong. I have so many people in my life right now who make me happy/healthy and strong and I am so thankful. I really love getting up, making my bed and starting my day that way-setting intention.

Something has really stuck with me from soul care Monday.

We often think of our future self at someone years from now, but in reality, our future self can be us 5 minutes from now.

How do you help create your future self? what are you doing now to support your future self?

even so much as waking up and making your bed, how that helps you feel through the day and sets you up for success at night.

I made a post before this one about how I specifically set up my weekly chiropractic visits for Thursday because I wanted to start off my morning with self-care and happiness on thankful Thursdays. Because for me, that feels good.

I started thinking what else makes me feel good and as I was hungry and wanted to indulge, I made a shaekology drink-because that makes me feel good. It makes me feel healthier, it makes me feel proud and accomplished and I enjoy starting my day this way and feeling this way.

How can you bring some happiness to your morning or day today?

What fills you with high vibrations?

This book journey has been a time of so many lessons and stories, that could honestly be a book in itself.

That is a book for another time.

How can you invest in your dreams today? (Money, Time, Energy...)

_____

_____

_____

_____

_____

_____

_____

_____

_____

SOURCE OF WELLNESS

1.7.21

I was invited to join open-source wellness through the native American health center (Oakland.) My counselor told me about it and it sounded like something that was in alignment with where I was at and where I was wanting to go.

Today is day 1.

We meet every week, once a day for 2 hours.

We check in, dance/stretch/move/exercise, have some focus on nutrition, time for mediation and even journaling, time for group coaching, we end by setting a specific goal and a tiny step to get there, we meet with the medical team, we get produce once a week from dig deep farms, we share gratitude's, victories and our goal for the week ahead

Today on day one we talked about why goals matter. To me goals matter because they keep us moving forward, they give us something to look forward to.

I love that in this group we talk about making smaller goals that are measurable and achievable.

I have been spending so much time, past few years trying to figure out who I am. Who I am outside of being a wife, a mom, a teacher? Trying to find my purpose outside of those titles and roles.

I spent all 2020 working on self-care, on claiming me, on creating habits and routines, on finding me again, putting me as a priority, trying new things, setting myself up better for 2021.

1.14.21

My goal is to design a life I love by doing more of what makes me happy. To say no to what doesn't serve me and say yes to what does. I am continuing to learn that self-care is not selfish. It is self-love. Right now, self-care and self-love look like getting outside, having yoga in the morning, intentional movement for 30minutes every day, journal daily, more water, better eating.

Some stuff is weighing me down: all that doesn't serve me, unused items/clothes/things, needing to

do too much at once-getting nothing done,
"schedule."
When I let go, I think I will feel more spacious,
room to design the life I love, I will feel
accomplished, flexible and have smaller goals.

1.13.21

I feel like I am being called to heal my family line.
I have always been called to break patterns, since I
was brought to life.
I am learning I can't heal anyone but me.
I am learning, I can help others by my own healing
and sharing my story.
I am being called to spend more time in nature.
I am re-writing the future, my future.

1.20.21

Everything in my home has earned its place
Everything that I have-has a story and purpose
and space.
Your thoughts are your story.
Whatever you think of my things, has nothing to
do with me.
What I think of what I have, has to do with me.
I feel like I see clutter but have a hard time letting
go. I have to figure out what no longer serves me.

I have to decide what's in alignment.
I've been conditioned to believe that I am a
hoarder.
That I have to have more in order to not feel poor.

The whole house is my nemesis
It isn't the visual and space I want right now, it's
not in alignment.
I am trying to create the space and welcome my
real identity
The mess doesn't bother me.
It only bothers me when it bothers other people
but I can be free to change when I let go of what
makes other people uncomfortable.
I am trying to design and create the life I love
That means I have to let go of some stuff.

2.2.21
I get to create the definition of my spaces. I want
to create certain feelings:
Safe, fun, chill, comfy, home, grounding, peaceful,
inviting.
My space can be chaotic, crowded, overwhelming,
filled and not private.
I am not sure who I was taught to be
But I am getting to know me and her story.

My phone and my book are pieces of my identity and story.
If there was a fire, what would you grab?
I feel like that is where your value is at.
Everything I am aligning with attracts my soul but takes practice to embody.

1.21.21
Today we talked about mindful eating, food being medicine: About eating with a purpose. About, eating to live but not living to eat.

1.28.21
I am proud of my first self-published book that went on sale this month. I am proud of so many things but this one I don't speak of enough because I don't want it to be a brag and I don't want the attention. But it truly means so much to my heart.
So today when asked what am I celebrating, I gave the answer I wouldn't have.
I am also proud of my kids in school, my loved ones sobriety, changing how my kids are growing up/how we are raising them. I am thankful to dream/not give up/have goals/self-healing and building relationships

I am thankful to celebrate me. I think it is important to celebrate ourselves and our accomplishments because it reminds us of our stories and that we can do so much, it reminds us to find the good in everyday and when we share- we help others feel brave enough to share or think differently. It is important to be seen, to witness others, to feel acknowledged and proud.
We don't celebrate ourselves enough because we have been taught its boastful, arrogant and narcissistic- so we minimize our things we should be proud of.
I will celebrate by speaking, by sharing, by writing, crying-even screaming

Someone told me that reflection is my superpower. And that they can see how my family is very important to me.
Our bodies aren't the same every day. I am happy we are reminded to do what feels good, today.

2.3.21
The most expensive thing I own is my life. My degrees, my time, my materials. I value myself and the quality of my life.

If I could do anything with my time I would be in Hawaii with my family, the trip would be paid for, a photographer would follow us around, no pandemic, no masks, space but less fears

I am so thankful for the open-source wellness program. I was a participant and a peer leader. Maybe one day I will become a coach, in this environment. Open-source wellness helped get me moving and to have fun while doing it. I ate the most veggies I have ever eaten. I spent time reflecting, journaling and being more mindful. I connected with others and built some relationships that have stayed even after our time ended in the program. Open-source wellness helped save my life in many ways. They helped me on the path I was yearning to be on, but is so easy to drift away from. Open-source wellness is a place I wish all people had access to.
For 8months of this year, I had this amazing program in my life.

Lena Ayala-Velasquez
July 15 · 21
Shared with Your friends

Open Source Wellness

opensource wellness has been in my life since January. I was brought the invitation to join through my counselor and it felt like the universe sent this to me. I knew I had to say yes because everything sounded like it was in alignment with who I was and who I was becoming. Open-source wellness covers everything that helps make life "better." We get moving (exercising while having fun) and everyone can feel safe to come as they are and still be "enough." I have found a group of people I look forward to seeing and hearing, a group of people who champion and support me. I have made connections outside of class to the people I have met in group. Open-source wellness is a beautiful community. I feel like I learn so much every time I show up. To be in this group of people is an honor. I have been a participant and now a peer leader and I am forever grateful.

My children and my family have seen me come out of my shell more and find myself more. I am learning about me through this experience, I am growing and I am happier.

Thank you to all of the coaches. They cover agreements, check ins, meeting with the medical team, making sure you get weekly food deliveries, meditation, teach about nutrition, share recipes, have coaching groups, offer opportunities for peer leaders, time to write and speak. Close with gratitude's, victories and declarations. Provide support and teach you how to make successful "goals."

I could keep talking but it will be way too long, I'll stop here but I hope so many get to experience what has been created here.

When you were a child, what did you want to be when you grew up? (Who do you want to be now?)

_____

_____

_____

_____

_____

_____

_____

_____

_____

_____

SOUL CARE

6.22.20

I have resistance, but-that is why I am saying
yes. "Inspired Possibility" Self-Care Sanctuary
with Barb Klein is group coaching. You do have
to pay. It feels like a risk, but I know it is worth
it. I know Barb is worth it. I know I am worth
it. I am thankful to Barb for reaching out to
me, again.

At first, I said "If my edd goes through today, I
will" but then I said "I actually have it now, so
why wait? Go for it. Money will come. What's
meant for me will be. This experience is
deserving either way, no excuses" and I paid.

6.22.20

I am thankful for my brothers and our
differences, I am thankful for my bed, what
our home will look like, and this group.
I am really trying to create and define my
relationship with self-care. I am re-defining it.

It is about honoring me, it isn't selfish. I am paying more attention about how I care for myself and the example I am being. I do not wish to create more burdens in my life, I am learning to say no when things do not feel like they are right for me. And I am learning to say yes when something calls to me.

I am learning everything is optional, and I have learned long before now that burn out is real...but more so lately, that it is not a "badge of honor"

I am in this phase of taking action on self-care, trying to be the best version of me. I am in many groups and practices lately. I am joining all things free that call to me. I am investing money which is new and big and scary and yet feels right to me. I am putting myself first, trying to keep me a priority because it's a new practice (as a mom) and I don't want that momentum to die down.

As I said I would take a break from groups- I felt my momentum and energy die down.

As I said yes to another group this morning- I felt myself saying yes more. Investing in myself – knowing I can, knowing it will serve me and its where I am meant to be -even if I don't know why.

As people introduce themselves in this group, I hear and feel different reasons why GOD has brought me here.

I am feeling emotional, tired, inspired and like I belong.

I need rest, to de-clutter, new set up, beauty, air and to journal.

I would love to travel. To serve others one day and get paid for it.

I am healing my relationships, my past, my soul, my mind, my home.

I am working on and wanting to create a night-time/morning routine. Sleep has always been hard for me. I am learning we have to digest everything we eat, see, hear and experience. I am learning what I do and don't want on my mind before bed (such as scrolling.) I am evaluating what will serve my sleep. And I am thinking about how I can start my days more intentionally.

My promise to myself for this next week is to get outside everyday intentionally and to short meditate every day.

If I can do all of this, I know it will all serve me
in the now and later.

I WANT YOU TO KNOW

I want you to know
You have never left
You have never been last
You have never left
I need you to hear this most
You don't need Facebook memories to know
You have grown but you have always been
You have never left
7/6/20

I AM NOT SURE...

I am not sure the last time I saw you
I am not sure the last time I was you
I am not sure it was ever even real

To me, enchantment shows me a forest
No phone to take pictures
No Facebook to check into

Moments pop in my mind
But none are pure delight

Some memories are delightful
Like great America, my children being born, the
nap I just took and becoming a teacher

I see you in moments of my children, and playing
games

What is pure delight?
What is delight?
What stops and interrupts delight?

I find happiness daily
Especially through the crazy

This morning with Jessica strong it was about
being a people pleaser
What that means, pretending, lying and
manipulating

Who am I without people pleasing?

I took time today to nap, to dream
What do I dream without trying?
What do I try to dream about?

What really matters to me?

What if that was what I let guide me?

I promise myself this week I will get outside, I will
be intentional about that
The last 4 days I haven't
I will get into nature
I will be an enchantment seeker

Taking care of myself
Takes care of everyone else

Because everyone else has to deal me
But first I have to deal with me
7/20/20

EYES CLOSED

If I keep my eyes closed, I will fall asleep
Would that still be meditation? Can we go that
deep?

This is the support I knew I needed
But I wasn't sure I'd get
I didn't know what to expect

I promise myself to be specific and real in my truth
and my story

I am very open and honest but to be specific has
the tears rolling
7/27/20

DISTRACTED

I found myself very distracted
And the times I wasn't- I was almost falling asleep
Why does meditation do this to me?

I am happy about being alive
About feeling my feelings and not asking them to
hide
I am happy about owning my thoughts
Allowing them to be instead of asking them to not
I am happy for this group called soul care
Even with all the happy, some things make me
scared

I am scared of letting go
Making changes, that change my world

Today I will give myself time, patience and a push
Today I will receive time, patience and flow
Today I most need to tell myself "Its ok to not be
done"
"it's ok that it is hard"
"it's ok to let go and change"

And now, I am peaceful
8/2/20

LETTER TO SELF

Write a letter to yourself, from the voice of
someone who loves you:

Dear mom,
If you could see what I see
You would see beauty
Beauty everyday
Any time of the day
You would see safety- you would feel safe
You would see intelligence
You know all the things
You know how to learn and grow and continue to
teach me
You would see, you.

I want to give you permission to:
Take time for you
Take time to rest
Take time not to clean
Take time to go on dates
Take time to not worry
Put the camera down

46

I want you to know
I love you unconditionally
You are a great role model.

What I love most about you:
Is how you care for me
How you are thankful
You are always here for me
You try to be fair

What I wish you knew
Is that its ok to love yourself
The way that you love me
I am ok

(Athena, kids and inner child)
"From the voice of someone who loves you"
At first, I had to question that. Husband, dad,
child, mom, Maddie, me?
8/3/20

8.7.20
I am longing for peace and zen. With reality. And
trust in change, to know it's not the end, it's not
over. And it can be better.

47

AWAKE AND AWARE

When I am awake and aware
I am intentional
I am flowing through life with untouchable peace
that brings happiness and all possibilities

Today I choose to shut off the social media news,
theories, pain and negativity
I choose to be present, get outside and be with
nature
I will find peace and ease my mind

I want to love this life
I want to enjoy
I want to be real and cautious
But I want the fear to stop shouting
I need it to calm down

I was born to be alive
To be change
I was born to be me
To be exactly who I am
And who I have been
Born to be true to me
(My husband sings born to be wild)
I am mom, teacher, wife, daughter, friend, student

Some of my gifts are: I am thoughtful, I am patient,
I am understanding, I am honest, I have integrity,
passion for writing, pictures of candid moments,

When I show up to life
Energies rise higher
People smile
People dig deeper
I feel happiness and peace
I know that anything is possible
I show up. Full. me. Real

I am...
I am here
I am alive
I am ready to grow
I am tuning into my body
I am awake
I am curious
I am hopeful
I am strong
I am human

I am so much more
Than just human

When I open my heart, to open my eyes
I find peace
I find myself wanting to take actions that my mind
will try to talk me out of
8/7/20

LOVE LETTER TO SELF

If you wrote a love letter to yourself, what would
love say?
Dear Lena,
How are you? How is loving yourself showing up
these days?
I want you to know, you are not too late. You are
right on time. Love is unconditional. Is that true?
Can you love without conditions? Allow love to
show up with acceptance. You do not have to
fight it or force it or change it.
Love you the way you love others.
Its ok to do that. It's necessary.

My invitation is to commit to
yoga/mediation/self-care.
8/7/20

8.10.20

Today I am happy to be here in soul care and for my unplanned day. I went with the flow. I am worried and scared about a 2-hour outing, mask time, Ikea crowd, not giving my kids enough me time.

Today I will give my house and my husband- attention and intention.

Today I hope to receive understanding from others and to myself.

Today what I most need to tell myself is "what didn't get done is ok."

It took me my whole life to get here, with self-care To be in coaching groups, that I paid money to be in

And still I sit here wishing there was a dads/men's group so that my husband could be a part of something so great also.

I am giving myself so much time but what about them? What about my kids and husband?

How is covid treating you? It's going. We get extra angel time, I am home with the kids, we moved right on time. We have help.

I am feeling like I am being selfish by consuming so much of my time with self-care. This group is a new level of vulnerability, honesty and support. It is so easy to put self-care on the back burner and feel like it's not ok when it is. I have to remind myself that self-care is ok.
Why does my self-care have to benefit you?
The baby didn't nap and dinner isn't ready-because I am here. Because of self-care.
What does that say about me? About my priorities? About my love for them? What am I making all of this mean?

8.17.20
Patience, honesty, positivity, writing and taking pictures
When I think of good qualities I have, I hear these words.
I don't need to soak them in because they are me
I want to acknowledge myself for my growth-I am constantly evolving.
I acknowledged myself for my documentation skills,
The way I am able to ground myself, the pictures I take that heal.

I can find happiness in every day, and I do
Every day I am happy-that is in fact true.
Today I am happy that I got Athena to nap before
soul care zoom
Today I am happy that I had lunch with my
husband, that I made the lunch too.
I am happy about iris getting the school supplies
she needs
That iris gets friend time, here and over there-that
I am more allowing of these things.
Being happy doesn't mean life is all good and
happy
I have fears, I have struggles, I get worried.
I am worried about upcoming conversations
I am worried about how scheduling will go when
sharing a child needs to be a conversation and
possible disagreement.
I am scared about my husband having a 7-day
work week
Days off matter, mental health matters, he matters
so much to me.
Today I will give, myself time to cook
I will give the kids time to sleep in and not over-
book.
I will give away iris doll house to someone we love

We will let go, it's been a hard road to get through the feelings and thoughts.
Today I will give, myself love and patience
I know that I need it and that others deserve it.
Today, I hope to receive rest
I hope to receive laughter, answers, peace and less stress.
What I need, isn't jumping out to me
I suppose balance, kindness and understanding.
Journaling and time alone to do so
Time outside, for us all -out of the house but right at home.
I want to promise myself that I will dig deeper
I want to dig deeper into the practices, questions, notes and quotes that are shared.

8/31/20

I saw the e-mail that tonight is our last session and I got sad
So, I took a nap. That's how I began to deal with that.
Last time we were together, I started to feel the end coming
I want to be able to connect outside of Monday meetings.

May I be self-compassionate
In this moment, may I be present.
May I feel all that is real and let it be ok
May I know it will all work out; it will all be ok.

I would like more support when it comes to
nutrition, fitness, date nights and de-cluttering
Making money and having a career is where I feel
pain and longing.

Today someone said to me
"I just want to be in your energy"
That really means a lot to me
I had to pause to really take that in, for me.

I feel like I can enhance my support network
I can start with making a vision board.
I can remain in this group, sign up and pay again
I can create a phone list; in case we lose this
connection.

Feeling like I can't do this again, financially
I consciously chose to invest in fitness, and I made
that priority.
Money coming in is less but still coming
Rent, bills, food, investments-all cost money.

Payment plans, scholarships
Do it or don't do it.
Celebrating myself for the investments made
I will be working on my fitness and writing my first
book, yay.
Some support groups have ended, due to covid
Like church and library time-two things I felt like I
needed.

Someone said to me "you are a light"
I promise to join the group again in the future, the
time will always be right.

My biggest take-away from this group series, is
many
All the faces and words, the connections and
feelings.
I am taking away the fact that I invested
I invested money, into something new, for me and
love it.
That has layers of take-aways
The smiles, the support, the comfort – there's no
way I can let this all go away....

9/14/20
New season, fall season

There will be 11 sessions.
I made it back to the group without a break
Year annual subscription is what I was able to pay.

Guard up but open
Faithful, patient and honest.
These are all qualities I like in others
Didn't realize they are in me already, what's to search for?

So many seedlings are being planted in me right now
To be more intentionally engaged and to get my fist book out.
In this moment I feel emotional, supported and happy
I need to cook and to be here- that's what I need.
I would love more blended family time
I would love, to go to Burney falls- I know we will in time.
I would love to live everyday like it's my birthday
I promise to be present and show up- for myself in every way.

9/21/20
Storytelling is important to me

I guess that's why I am always documenting.
My journey matters to me
My creativity, my truth, my dreams.
It's so much more than a blog or Facebook post
There's so much more to it all, whether you do or
don't know.
I am a healer, I have always been
I am a facilitator, by choice or by being chosen.
I tell my story and I tell the story of others
Everyone's story matters.
I am still figuring out all of my stories
There's so many layers and pieces of me.

I have stories I feel I must tell
My daily life, I like to share.
I want to tell the story of being a step mom
Of being a coparent, and being a mom.
The stories of my family
Being a wife and daughter – of loving those who
suffer addictions, situations that changed me.

I don't share for the sake of sharing
I don't write just for the sake of writing.
I share, for my own healing
I share, for my own memory.
I share, in case someone else can relate

I share, in case someone else can befit from what I
have to say.
I share-the good and the bad
I share, to help others feel like they can share too-
that its ok to be real.
I write, because it's a release for me
I write, because it's my therapy.
I write because it's a part of who I am
I write because, I can.

9/28/20
I am tripping over a few things today
Resting, sleeping, naps, sleep---I guess it's more
like one common theme
I hear my future self-talking to me today
Telling me it's just as good to rest, even if it's not
sleep.
It's just another story that I am changing
I am constantly growing.

Doing things together, doing it all
Money struggle.

The movie trolls is on my mind
We can have it all, maybe not all of the time.
But we can have it all

Fun, entertainment, dance, lyrics-all.
You don't have to be just one thing
I am human and I am made up of so many things.

My body wants to get out and go on a walk
My body wants to feel the fresh air, it would love
sleep and a massage.
My body feels tired
It wants me to know it is strong and holding a
lot....

9/30/20
My life revolves around others
I am a wife; I am a mother.
I am a daughter, a sister, a friend
I am a teacher, a worker, a part of someone's
equation.

Self-care can no longer be another thing on the to
do list
Self-care can no longer revolve around others and
me not even being someone important.
In this moment I feel tired and the want to get
active
I need a nap and family time-even a bike ride.
I would love to meet the women of soul care

What do I most need to hear?
Right now, I need to hear "try it"
I am hearing the whispers of melatonin.
I am hearing that my dad is with me
That the book will be "perfect" as in it will feel
complete.

What really matters to me right now
Is to de-clutter, to let go and throw out.
To start family game nights or family cooking or
both
To have more mediation, yoga, rest, journaling and
outside time.
I want less time on social media
I want less time on my phone.

Months ago, I would not have made time for me in
this way
Anything is possible, I know that even more today.
I made it through the time of being on zoom with
a group of soul care sisters
Months ago, I wouldn't have been able to imagine
having time for me in this way-I would have said it
didn't matter.

10/5/20

Someone in group said to me that I am a good
mom
It broke me, I don't always feel like a good mom.
You barley know me, so you know not what you
speak of
You barley know me, how do you see this in me?
How can you say this with such love?

I am writing my first book, about my dad
I feel good to feel safe to say and own that here
with you all -been awhile since I have felt that.
Do I talk about it before its real?
I feel ok to do that here.

10/12/20

Thoughts of yesterday are still very real
Asking for our oldest for my birthday and feeling
all there is to feel.
The feelings, the surrender
It's packaged that way-can't have one without the
other.

So much other stuff on my mind
Coparenting is just one aspect of my life.

There's also loving the ones I love who are dealing
with addictions
There's also the past I have with parents who
dealt with alcoholism.
There's sickness loved ones are fighting
There are the stories I have of realities.

10/12/20
I am working on letting go sooner
I am not enjoying the feelings of anger.
If I stay angry, I will miss out on the day
If I stay angry- it won't go away.
Anger makes me miss out on what's good
My anger projects onto others and that negative
energy does no one any good.
If I stay angry...I will ruin all of us
I need to let go, for me, for them-for all I love.

10/12/20
When I was an acorn, what was inside of me?

Am I now the oak tree?
Those little acorns, now grow on me?
Did I grow from that seed?
Or, am I still growing, constantly?

I have grown a lot, a lot more yesterday than in
the last 14 years
It has taken me so much to surrender to the pain,
anger and fears.
To surrender, rather than fight
To pause worry, so that I can enjoy all that is right.

I don't want to take away from me anymore
So, I surrender.

10/19/20
You can have covid fatigue and still live life
Are you wondering what that looks like?

I have so much I am working on
On surrender, acceptance- the list goes on.
I really want to live everyday like it's my birthday
To celebrate every day in this way.

This year was supposed to be different for my
daughter
We were looking forward to having her brother
here for her birthday + the day before and after.
We were looking forward to the weekend since a
year ago
This opportunity is rare, don't you know?

No need to ask for permission
School here, with no time limit.

Whose karma is this?
How do I practice peace through all the emotion?

To practice living in the moment
Even if it isn't what I wish
Even if incomplete
How is this our reality?

Reality that he won't be here for any of this
Because, sometimes-life just happens.
Because we are living in a pandemic
And rules apply to this uncharted territory of this
new experience.

Don't let the pain, fear and grief-
Takeover, all of these days to be.
We can still be productive, we are still blessed
We will make the most of this.

I have come far with my response, acceptance and
reactions
I have come so far, uplifting others and allowing
my emotions.

It's not a good day
But it's not a bad day.

I'm sitting with it
With the facts and feelings and emotions.
But I refuse to hold on to the doom
I already know what that path would do.

10/19/20
The angels want...

Me to live in my purpose and practice my beliefs
I am being tested and I felt it coming.

Angel wants to be here, he was so ready
Ready for the celebrations and rare opportunity.
Angel wants to be here; he was looking forward to
the extra time
And now we get none of that- we are losing so
much time.

The angels want...
Me to flourish
To take this time, to nourish me.

10/26/20
Writing is my hobby
Writing is my passion, my therapy-my healing.

I would love to know how this book touches others
Imposter syndrome tells me, who am I to touch others or claim myself as an author?

I forgive myself for, not speaking up
For not pushing myself and allowing me to give up.
I forgive myself, for letting myself quit
For projecting my feelings on to others, knowing they didn't deserve it-even if they "did".
I forgive myself, for judging others
I like to think I don't, but I know I do and I am working on noticing more.
I forgive myself, for not letting go
For holding on to things that don't serve me and only hurt my soul.
I forgive myself, for assuming
I forgive myself for, for forgetting.
I forgive myself for not making the time
For losing the mom that I once was, for changing over time.

I forgive myself, for not taking the job
For not being able to protect, those and what I
really love.

Does forgiving mean I won't do it again?
If I, did it again, does that mean I don't mean all of
this?

I appreciate myself, for speaking up
I could be silent many times, but instead I don't
bite my tongue.
I appreciate myself, for responding instead of
reacting
For trying new things.
I appreciate myself, for listening to my body
For listening to my intuition, for surrendering.
I appreciate myself, for feeling and dealing
For holding on when I want to let go, for not
forgetting.
I appreciate myself, for having patience
For asking all the questions -when I have
questions.
I appreciate myself, for making the time
For investing in me, to be better for them and
better for myself-this time.

I appreciate me, for committing to chiropractic
care
For seeing what commitment can mean, knowing
the life without it there.
I appreciate me, for being home with the kids
For learning and growing and being honest.
I appreciate myself, for writing
For writing a book, for smiling.

My promise to myself is to put my all into this
book I am writing.
Thankful to be able, to speak about my dad-
without crying today. To speak here, in this group
about him and about this book. With a smile and
not just pain.

11.2.20
Deep down inside....

Deep down inside, I don't know what sickness I
may or may not have
I know my past shows I get sick easily and long
lasting
I know my past shows how strong my mind is
Manifestation is me
I used to see it as a curse

But now I have learned- differently
I'm no witch like I thought as a child
I am spiritual, powerful and capable-that is me

Deep down inside, I am scared
Scared of failing and succeeding
I am stalling
I am thinking too much

Deep down inside,
What is deep down inside?
Can I go that deep?
What will I hear?
What will I feel?
What will I see?

What do I seek?

Deep down inside
I am unsure
I am for sure
But I play in the un-decisive
Knowing I can have it all
So why not just go with it?

Either way, will lead me right

(This didn't flow, it wasn't poetry. I had to keep asking the prompt-to not get distracted. I kept finding myself distracted, wanting to think- instead of just write. What happens if I just write? Saying the prompt each time would lead me to somewhere different and new.)

I promise to not live-in regret
The time is now
But it is also ok to rest
To change the plans, if they bring stress

11/9/20
I am feeling drained. I need and want sleep.
I am feeling worried.
Worried about the cold, fear of us getting sick
Counseling was great this morning, up until the questions.
The questions about childhood, made me emotional
It's been hard to shake the feelings

I make my bed for my future self
The me that loves to get into a nice bed at night.

For the me who loves to see the bed at peace and happy.
Today has been frustrating.
The book process and everything is getting to me

11/12/20
If I was a vegetable, I would be an avocado
I know it's a fruit but many think it's a vegetable
I love to debate, I love to research
I love to question and even rebel
They call it "good fat"
And, who can't use more of that?
Indecisive and confusing- that can definitely be me
Good either way-there's always positivity-
especially within the hard things
It can go with sweet foods or not
Its good alone, or not
It can be expensive or free
If I could be a vegetable.... avocado is what I would be

11/12/20
The holiday season is different, because of the pandemic
Is it? Is it limited? Is it restricted?

Or is it all clearer?

The holiday season, is about family and new
traditions
It's about being incomplete sometimes and
sometimes not- it's all about perspective
It means time off of school and work
Holiday seasons can mean money stress
It's about reframing the thoughts that come with
It's about making it what I want it to be
I want it to be memorable memories

I want it to be memories, that I want to remember
Now I am reflecting on growing up and the past
few years
What will it look like this year or in the future?
This year is in the future

What really matters and what have you been told
it "Should be"
Expectations, obligations, reminding and
connecting.
Re-thinking, simplifying, re-newing and
commercialism
Who makes the rules? You do! You just haven't
noticed

You can create it all differently
"That won't happen" can be what happens, if you
want it to be.
Flow with it, go with it
Don't set yourself up for disappointment

You can't regain what's no longer there
The past is the past, now is right here.

Covid is the built-in excuse
You don't have to see the family you don't want
to.
You don't have to live the stories you are used to
You don't have to fear the substance abuse.
Finances don't need to be the worry
Shopping for gifts is in fact voluntary.
You don't have to choose anxiety
You can create the holiday of your dreams.

11/12/20
Self-care is....
 Rest
and doing what will bring me happiness.
Its doing what will bring me peace
Self-care is flowing, not forcing anything.
If it brings stress then I will ask why

I will ask is it necessary and how can I change it to
be the opposite of a stressful time.
Self-care is learning what serves me
And using my voice to speak up when I feel the
need to say anything.
Giving myself permission to know I am deserving
Deserving of my freedom of speech.
Self-care is treating myself with the same love,
thoughtfulness and respect that I give to others

I used to think self-care was manicures and
pedicures
Getting my eyebrows done and buying the things I
wanted but I have changed and am proud of it.

To get to my own self-care, I had to do it by
saying "this will help everyone else. I will work on
me to better take care of everyone else" because
that was my way to justify, that is what I believed.
That is what it was.
Now I know taking care of me still make everyone
else happy. And I am leading by example.

My self-care doesn't have to be or mean: making
everyone else happy
Gratitude saved me.

Every time I complain- it reminds me of gratitude.
It could be better, but it could be worse too.
I need gratitude to get through

11/16/20
Fears of feeling sick, getting sick and the
judgement
They are big feelings, don't treat me like I have
covid
I would be this way and do this with any sickness
Not exactly, there is now an extra layer of fear
and conditions

I am fearing my child will her themselves
Because they are feeling judged and I don't know
how to help
Do we send everyone else away?
How do we all behave?

We are allowed to have sickness
For it to be normal, like before covid pandemic
We are also allowed to be honest
To be open about our thoughts and emotions that
we are dealing with
We are allowed to be different
To love each other and still need to process

Life can get too dark too fast
Isolation can be more harmful than protective
Right now, pandemic rules aren't healthy for me
Right now, I need to be mommy

11/23/20
I am a woman of my word
I am a woman of many words
I am afraid to do wrong
My intentions are not that
I am a rule follower-unless I need to fight back
I like to play fair
I do have other sides of "beware"
I am honest, I try to practice all I preach
I am inspired, constantly

These wrinkles are from 32 years of life
These gray hairs don't bother me enough to be
colored otherwise.

My inner misfit, says I'm no misfit at all
I am fighter
I do not like injustice
I do not like unfair

I release fear, professionalism
I release the old me

I claim to live in my brave
To get uncomfortable until I reach my comfort I
want

My light, is bright-even when dimmed
I may shine my brightest in those moments
My light sometimes flickers and I have to find my
way- to not go out completely

But its ok, its ok to rest
If it's dark-that's what's happening

I release the fear, but I haven't claimed it

11/23/20
I am proud of myself for wanting to include others
For chasing my dreams and living what matters
I am proud of myself for wanting to honor and
respect others

12/7/20
In this moment, I am happy
I am happy to have my family.

I am happy to have support groups
I am happy to know my husband's test results.
I am happy to have soul care.

In this moment, I am worried and concerned about
positive covid test in our house
I am worrying about the "how"
How will the kids and I and we all do fighting this?
I feel tired and scared and some regret
My soul wants me to know that peace will come
through and I will be at peace
My soul wants me to know, all is as it should be

I promise to focus on positives and allow all
feelings
To tap into the support, I and we need

12/14/20
A part of me is positive
A part of me is untouchable
A part of me is realistic
A part of me is unstoppable.
A part of me feels strong
A part of me is powerful
A part of me feels wrong
A part of me feels vulnerable.

A part of me feels tired
Knows I am fighting a sickness that has taken
many lives and damaged many others.
A part of me is afraid
Afraid to feel this part of me too much
Afraid for it to be too real

Last Monday my husband got his positive results
And in that we all got the same news
My soul wants me to know right now that this is
not over
This fight, this journey- my story
And its ok to rest
It is ok to not feel well or have to be at my best.

What is my soul telling me?
Why isn't it clear to me?

Do I pay $1000 for medicines and use our rainy-
day funds
Do we need the money or is this what savings are
for?
We are a week into this, I should have invested
sooner
It will take days to get here.

Is it worth it this late?
Am I thinking too much?

I need to remember is that what matters most is
that life is short
What matters most?

C19 is not a joke
Illness is not a joke

When you know better
You have to do better

So, what do I know?
What should I be doing differently?

The gifts that you have to give
Only you can give

12/21/20
What is alive for me right now is my dreams
To dream and make them reality.
To rest and to live out loud
To go big and have hope and make others proud.
To surrender, embrace and leap into courage
To know, no matter what-it will all be worth it.

I am embracing being an author
Working on how to bring in income and what
comes after

Standing at the peak, I can't help but smile
And feel like, anything is possible.

A sigh of relief...
Yep, that's for me.

Release...
Honoring my journey

There are still more peaks to come
This is just one

I acknowledge myself for where I have invested
money, time and myself
This year I found church in me, in home, it's not a
specific place but more like what's felt

I found my vision and my drive
I have let go...differently this time
I have made dreams real
I have put me first and continued to heal

I am proud and celebrating
New income opportunities
More angel time, involved with school and life
Covid time off and support felt so nice

2020 has been the year of anxiety release
Continued depression healing

I want to leave behind fear, doubt, worry and
perfectionism
I want to leave behind scarcity mindset,
compassion, burn out and imposter syndrome.

I want to take with me, courage confidence and
clarity
I want to take with me light fun and peace.
I want to take flow with me
I want to take a morning and nighttime routine,
that feels good to me.
I want to take exercise habits
I want to bring faith, warmth and vision.
I want to bring with me- patience and being
present
I want to take with me- intention.

I want to experience and feel -more hope, peace,
play and fun
I want to travel more-in 2021

12/21/20
This year I took all the bad and found the good

I had to give myself permission to be ok with
feeling good when the world was crashing and so
many felt worse than not good

I learned that putting me first doesn't mean I don't
care for everyone else

Putting me last doesn't actually make me happy or
show my love more

Does my new year have to be a sister?
Just because this year wasn't

I lived out my themes
I lived in my dreams

How can the next year compare?
I am more scared
And hoping it can only get better

But part of me is barley holding the positivity
together.

I feel guilty with how good I feel
Putting me first doesn't mean I love them less

I don't want to feel ashamed by the goodness I
feel

12/21/20
Perhaps, for a moment
It can be ok to not be ok
It can be ok, to not be ok
Perhaps, for a moment-and always
I can live in my truth without shame
I can live out loud knowing all will change
But I can let each moment be what they will be
I can surrender to what is and be free
I can live life without comparison
I give myself permission

My promise to me
Is not to lose me
To continue to flow
And implement the way of life I dare to dream and
now know

12/28/20
What's alive for me right now is tiredness
Fear of long haul, feeling those symptoms
News of another loved one's death near
Fear of fear
My mind is busy and groggy
Pain in my body
Week long leg pain
Lower back pain Christmas eve and day

I should ...be, thankful for sobriety
For the men I love who mean so much to me
For a holiday without alcoholic drinks
For the answered prayers, finally.

Physically I woke up tired and in pain
I did all the things that make me happy but yet it
didn't change
I didn't let the cold keep me in
I took a nap but woke up to be present
I know my body wants more rest
I feel like I feel hot but I didn't want to miss out on
this.

This year I have loved time

Time with myself
Time with loved ones
Time outside

I loved what money has given me
Dressers, desks, matching furniture and coaching
Certificates, oils and candles
Jeans and things that make me feel beautiful

I have lost...faces, that I love-know and knew
I have lost attachment- to people, places and
things too
I have lost some old stories
I have lost so much...but also found me
Found my purpose

1/4/21
I am just flowing with it
With life and all of the moments

Self-care to me is doing what makes me happy
Its clay masks and working out-even drinking tea.
It's getting outside, getting massages, waxes and
doing my nails
Its journaling and sharing-everything that's real.

Soul care to me is a feeling
Soul care to me, is what brings my being peace.
It's what lights me up inside
It can be different things at different times.
It's when I feel like my best self
When I can live as my higher self.

Imagine yourself at the end of 2021
What have you done?

I am driving
We have a new car, I am teaching
I wrote two more books
We have traveled

I think to 5 years from now
I can experience future happiness right now
I am going to make it all real
Its already mine, that's just how I feel
5 years I am unsure
But this year, I know for sure
It all makes me smile, now
I am completing my vision board to help me out.
I am continuing to work on me
Doing what matters to me

Family, safety, happiness and peace
Those are all truly important to me
Nature, calm, living
That all matters to me

I heard that being happier adds years on to your
life
Then Marlene says "I'm going to live today like I'm
alive"

1/11/21
Part of me is in pain
My back, my head- all I feel is the pain.
Part of me is tired
Part of me danced and part of me smiled.
I even laughed through the music
Part of me is overwhelmed with plans and goals-
the unknowns and to do list.
Part of me is chill, going with the flow
Part of me feels behind, the year just started-I
know.
Part of me is celebrating
My brother's birthday, life, food and family.

I am grateful, I am hopeful and full
I am cold, I am warm and even playful.

Sad, grief, loss, scared
It all lives here.

1/25/21
I am cold
I am enjoying this book/author journey
I have so many thoughts, so many
I need to spend time reflecting deeper
A friend asked about the healing groups I am in
and if I can be her counselor.

2/1/21
Soul care right now looks like, things I'm wanting
to do are getting done
I feel alive, I feel good
I am noticing my energy flow
I am noticing what matters to me most

The purpose of my life is to live
To help others live
To make this world better
To be me, to show up-to be honest and real.
To create change
I do not have just one purpose, I have many.

To be a mom and wife

I cherish time
I cherish making others happy
I cherish memories and creating memories
I cherish my family
I cherish my writing.
I cherish my time to reflect
I cherish relationships

If anyone could grant me my hearts deepest desire
It would be to live; I have many wants and desires.
My intention to be happy aligns with this
Its helping me live
To be present
And intentional in every moment

I am doing
I am implementing
I am trying
I am forward moving.

Today someone told me they appreciate my heart
That I mirrored back to them-so much truth,
honesty and healing and love.

If I stay with the seeds I am planting now
Then in 6-12 months I will feel happy and proud.

It will look fulfilled and accomplished
I will have written more books and stayed in my
magic
I will be wiring more and touching more lives
May I be open to the compliments, the love, the
support, the changes of time
My promise to myself is to show up for me the
way my heart desires
How did I get to be who I am-is a question and
story that matters

2.8.21
I will show up more true to myself
By following my hearts and writing books that will
one day be on a shelf
I will connect with more family
And I will speak honestly

So much is possible for me
While finding my dad, I am finding me

Right now, so much is challenging me
My fears, my pain, my doubt and the unknown
future telling

I am feeling happy about answering calls

I feel proud for connecting with others, listening
to my heart and our book

I want to acknowledge myself for showing up
For speaking up
I am cultivating patience, giving, honesty,
commitment and courage-these days
This group and everyone it in plays a role in how I
show up these days

I have several words for this year
Courage, courageous, acceptance, connection,
gratitude and surrender

2/15/21
My fire...

My fire has sparks
My fire doesn't like the dark
So, it stays lit
Even if its small, so small you can barely feel it
It's always there
It raises high the more I care

I do enjoy good company
I love to bring those I love with me

(campfire)
My fire procrastinates
But the other part of me -yells "why wait?!"
(2nd book)

I love fire
The beauty, the crackle, the warmth and company
Sometimes I need help to get the burn started
Even help to keep it going
Even help to put it out
Why force it out? I won't, I don't
I just let it go

2/15/21
My eyes are tired, my shoulders are tight
I want to stretch-to feel alright

I found my fire
And I'm getting tired
How do I match my fire?
I need to allow myself to be tired...to rest

I need to recharge
So, I can take charge

Do I keep going? I want to do more

I want to rest also

2/15/21
What matters to me that I don't want to miss
Is time with my kids
When they want to talk or play or cook or eat
When they ask for time with me/from me
When my husband wants time, dates and cuddle
with me
Everything is connected for happiness and peace

I will allow myself to prioritize rest
So that I can find my fire again

I won't focus on how much I will miss this group
the next two week
I will focus on how exciting it will be when
returning

3/7/21
That inner critic is repetitive
Telling me I can't change and can't afford "it"
That inner critic looks grumpy, unhappy, tired and
hurt
That inner critic is just lost, processing, finding her
healing and feeling all the feelings

That inner critic is ok as is
My mood of today, right now-all affects this

My inner critics job is here to keep me safe
To keep me playing small-to challenge me
To help me find courage and action to take
To stay comfortable or get uncomfortable-
whichever is calling

My wise self is sadness. My inner critic will help
guide and coach me through this.
As you are
Prayer hands
I can make space for it all

Inner critic isn't good or bad, just is
There's no power over me-just acceptance

3/22/21
My soul is feeling satisfied today
Also tired wanting rest to accomplish more of
what I crave

For this time, I just need and want to be here
To be present and see what happens for me here

I feel tired
I need to do more
I want to know more

3/22/21
My super powers are hearing people
Championing people
Observing
Caring for others
Being honest and open

I'm hearing people talks and I'm translating it into questions

Poetry flows from me but I never want that to be an expectation

Someone told me "You are memorializing our words
I love how you capture our quotes Lena, thank you"

3/29/21
In this moment
I am so much "better" than this morning
I am feeling rested without napping

I feel tired but calm
In this moment I am happy to be here, even
though my husband is home
He even sold one of my books to a coworker
I am surprised and happy and still here

I am breaking free
From old ways, past traumas, old stories
I am grateful for courage, growth and me

4/5/21
When I show up for my life
My uncle says I have the Garfield smile
I enjoy who I see in the mirror

4/12/21
Self-care for me has looked like, getting more
sleep
Having routines
Diving into my passion of book writing
Learning what feels good and what doesn't serve
me
Sleep, food, outside time
Money, to do lists, flowing with life.

For self-care I do many things

Clean my space, write, sleep
Create meaningful alarms, brush my teeth
Open curtains, open windows, participate in yoga
and coaching
Shower, not wear a mask
Go on walks, see the chiropractor -even get my
nails done

I am taking each day as its own
I am proud not to get the shot right now and not
have the kids in school
Finding work from home
Being out of masks as much a s possible

Knowing my priorities and boundaries
It all means so much to me

I'm doing this, for me
Cause it's better for me
And that makes me better

4/19/21
"left-over Lena"

I am showing up with what's left of me

What's left over from today's situations and
happenings

I'm not home, I am joining from family's house
I am using someone's space and technology now

I am fearing so much stuff
Stuff that I don't feel safe to speak of
In this book, not in this group
But money is one of the issues
New car finances too
I'm emotional its true

Athenas voice is "out"
Leo missed some school

Some loved ones are willing to risk what I am
unsure of
I am only in control of me, I can speak my
concerns but I also have to be ok with choices that
aren't mine

We didn't get good news, but at least its honest
It's not news we hoped for but at least we are
finally hearing something

Whatever happens is what needs to happen-in order to move forward
It's always steps in the right direction-even when I am unsure

I know what happiness looks and feels like
But I can't get there right now, in my mind
But I do know it

Happiness feels and looks like so many things to me
Energized, strong, fun, calm and possibilities
Adventurous, positive, satisfied and peace
Content and calming

4/26/21
I am mad about procrastination and clutter
I am sad about masks and being tired
I am sad about yelling
I am sad about the cost of lawyers to help with certain things
I am glad about gratitude
I am glad about having a home to go home to
I am glad about family
I am glad about my author journey
I am glad about getting outside today

I am glad about peer leadership, yoga and faith.
I am hopeful for the world "normalcy"
I am hopeful of this book journey
I am hopeful for the future of our blended family
I am hopeful to, getting more sleep.

I want to be hopeful

5/3/21
I think of summer and I think of heat which means
flies inside
It means no screens on the door or windows, so
we won't just be letting air inside
It means spilled ice cream and things
Which means ants will come abundantly
It means mosquitos which means bites
It means allergic reactions, medicines and fears of
illness
It means sunburns if you want to have fun in the
sun
It means dehydration

Some of us woke up snotty
Some of us have known allergies
Our oldest got all of his siblings' gifts

Wrong times for my husband's lunch brough on
frustrations
I am making gifts for people I love
I am so thankful for yoga

5/3/21
Love helps me understand
Love helps me see from different perspectives
Love is not pain-pain is not love
Love just is-love is above all
Love comes easy to me, through me and for
others
Love is for me-from me and doesn't depend on
others
I used to love to be loved
I let it define so much
...I used to think so differently
I guess that's what love has done for me

I promise to love myself a little bit more this week
I will do this by honoring/respecting and listening
to me
To my heart and intuition
This also means getting more sleep, creating that
action

Putting the phone down and getting to bed is the intention
I also promise to get a pedicure with my husband

And I will continue to meet myself where I am

5/17/21
I would like to acknowledge myself for, getting the baby to sleep
Sticking to my schedule even though others have opinions they shared with me
I am doing what's best for me and my family
I am doing what works for me
Naps work for her, for me-for all of us
When she naps-we all win

I am grateful for my mom getting us groceries
I am grateful for where we live
I am grateful for last year- all of the dreams that are now reality

I am struggling with trusting money will come
I am struggling with momentum
I am struggling with my purpose and my path
I am struggling with knowing it will become more clear-even though I know that

I am struggling with the covid rules that are ever
changing
I am struggling with the masks and shots -the
changes of life that are moving so quickly

My soul needs truth, trust, clarity and peace
I am thankful I know what helps me relax when I
am feeling upsetting feelings
Writing, quiet, reflecting
Revisiting, speaking up, a shower, a nap- feeling
the feelings
I am thankful I know what supports and nourishes
me through the day
Like yoga, water, getting outside and writing what
I have to say

When I am in a good mood
There are things I like to do
I like to write and be with others
I like to eat, sing, dance and do those things by
myself or with others

5.29.21
I am getting so clear on the boundaries around
health that matter to me

Not because someone is telling me what it has to
be
I am learning from going within
I am learning to trust my intuition

Right now, people care about who's vaccinated,
who's not
Who's masking, who's not
Who's this or that-and then they can take action
around that
Then they can place judgement
I'm not into it

6.7.21
Gratitude through my body
Feels necessary for me
It feels like more calm, more peace
Literally

I have been feeling off and allowing it to be
Allowing me to be
Surrendering to being open, confused, flexible and
in flow- with grace
I am signing up for things and feeling in to the
feelings they create

The summer I desire involves traveling
With no masks and with family
It looks like new experiences
Maybe crossing some things off the wish list
It looks like no more school
And my husband taking time off of work, to have
a break too

I desire sun, heat, laying on the ground
My feet in the sand, listening to the ocean sound

Date weekends and maybe a getaway
Dedication to yoga, almost everyday
Time outside
I want real life
Time away from screens
Time in reality

It looks like monthly massages and getting my
nails done
It looks like doing those things alone or with
someone

It looks like being present with the kids
Drinking more water, writing more and playing big

I desire flow, prosperity, clarity and purpose
The summer I desire, can and does exist

6.7.21
I don't think anything can get in the way of
acknowledging gratitude
But I am human, I do have my moods
Deep pain, anger and not understanding
Those feelings can get in the way of gratitude for
me
However-reflection, being alive and checking in
with myself in the moment-helps
Sometimes its going outside, sometimes it's a nap,
sometimes music or a shower-helps
Gratitude comes with so many benefits
Clarity, peace-even happiness
It's a ripple effect
I am grateful for so much, in every moment

I am grateful for even the fears, worry and
hesitance
It all serves a purpose, it all benefits

6.21.21
The summer I desire, would not involve in person
summer school

It wouldn't involve any school
I want to travel to places on my list
LA, Yosemite, Burney Falls and weekend date trip
We have already made it to Redding with family
We have already made it to Santa margarita for
celebrating

I have been easily distracted and easy to give up
When it comes to yoga, not drinking soda,
exercise, routine of sleeping/waking up
I am tired
I am awakening to my dreams, little by little
I am re-defining
I am reflecting
Back to the height of last year, some of the goals
and challenges
I am tired, there's no denying it

The light within me, comes in waves
Sometimes bright
Sometimes dim
At times leads the way
And at times, can't be found

When I embody and apply myself

To yoga, living my dreams, traveling, sleeping,
outside time, exercise, drinking water and doing
my nails
It all nourishes me
Getting my eyebrows done, doing face masks,
taking time to write and read
Its different things daily
It's a lot of checking in with me

I trust, I will find my way
That it will all work out and it is already-everyday
Everything is as it should be
I will continue to find myself – no one can do it for
me

I intend to find peace and comfort this summer
With and for, the next school year
Whatever that ends up being for us
...in the unknown I trust

I am, ready to use my voice
To always know I have a choice
I am open to receiving
Willing to change and do reclaiming

Learning doesn't have to be done in the classroom

I know that, I've lived that and yet I get scared too
I came into this year more scared than of last
Wondering and worried how I can compete with that
Knowing I don't have to but wanting to live up to or beyond
And yet I am not....

When I open my heart to who I am right now, I know I am who I need to me
And I am where I am meant to be
I know I am a work in progress
And yet I am most complete while in the process

When I open my heart to who I am right now, I am living the way I choose
I have power, I know I do
I get to create my future and past
I get to learn as I look back

I know I am whole
I am human and I have holes
But that just means there's room for growth
That just means, it's all natural

I will always be a teacher

I will always be a mother

I am a leader, from behind the scenes
I think it may be time to take the stage-no more strings
I have the power to create change and not settle

I look to my inner child for guidance
She is me; I am she and we are becoming into alliance

I promise to pause, and enjoy today
While not allowing next school year to work me up before then and get in the way

I want to plan
But so much can change by then

I know how I feel
Where do I have power still?
Where am I willing to settle?
Where do I have boundaries that aren't changeable?

7.5.21

So many practices are supporting me right now in
my daily life

Its all moment by moment, if I'm being honest – its
all a practice and takes time

I have practices I want to create

I have been attending yoga most days

I attend courageous life society on Wednesdays

I write daily and give thanks

I drink more water and I cook more

I attend soul care and put the phone down more

I go to sleep earlier and wake up earlier than
before

I am getting outside more and more

Someone told me that pain is inevitable but
suffering is optional

Fear, anger. Shame and guilt-have taken its toll

To love myself and care for myself more

I am going to hold boundaries that matter

I am going to flow

I am going to be present

7.19.21

It's a beautiful thing when you have a group to
check in with every so often
Although promises haven't been on my mind, I
notice I have been living it all during reflection
When I look back on my notes, I know
It feels good to just live without too much thought
process to hold

I am re-framing all of my stress and annoyances
Thank you neck and body pain- you made me put
me first and finally make a chiro appointment
Thank you to our 3-year-old for screaming to let
me know you were upset
Thank you, patience, for allowing me to give her
that time she needed
Thank you, permission, to myself to be in yoga and
breathe though
Thank you for allowing it for her too

Thank you inner voices for guiding me
Thank you to me, for listening
Thank you to me for trusting the unknown
And for allowing myself to watch it all unfold

7.19.21

I am honoring the moments
To be bitter or not, it's all about perspective

Its about the battle vs the war
Who and what really matters more?
I can go down either road
This time I want peace more

Writing is how I process
Complaining helps me find gratitude

8.2.21

We listened to "we can do hard things" by Tish
Melton

That song made me emotional
I can relate on so many levels
We may not mean the same things
And yet we can connect and feel similarly

I am constantly coming out on the other side
I chose my battles last night
I went in with no intention to fight
I had already made up my mind

Your words of hurt no longer boil me over
Revisiting the past, lives here-no longer
I can re-visit without going back
I no longer live in the past

I can put myself in your shoes
But I refuse to feel guilty for not sharing the same truths

8.2.21
I am allowing ease in with flow
I am allowing trust in the unknown
I am feeling all of the feelings
I am choosing to respond over reacting
I am bringing in ease when it comes to my intentions
Honesty allows for me to have peace within
I am allowing me to be me
No agenda, no force- just imperfect and free
I am allowing my story to be told
Allowing "real" to be easy and let the rest unfold

8.2.21
There are some burdens I am carrying that are not mine to bear

Like being a mom and making/allowing "stepmom"
and other peoples feelings to take away from that
just because a child is shared
Kids school decisions
Not "working" and needing the income
Not having books done and not driving
It depends on how it affects me

When I carry these burdens, I don't like who I am
I am tired, I am stressed, sad, emotional and
broken

If I released these burdens, I think I could love me
I would feel empowered, peaceful and free

8.2.21
Some ease comes with burdens
Its easier to do hard things when I am speaking for
the voiceless
When I am helping those speak up, who can't
alone
I can be brave and courageous for them, for my
kids

Yesterday was hard on me, on we

And yet I loved how I was able to handle it so differently

Your stories about me, are not my Burdon to carry
Moving on, apologies and understanding – don't always mean it goes away because of those things
It also doesn't mean I have to keep it just because you get carried back
I don't have to relive it with you, I don't have to agree or compromise when I don't mean it
I don't have to please you or share your mindset

I need to be me
Tell my story with honesty

Your pain, your truths, your anger-are not mine to carry
Your reactions are not mine and they do not serve me

8.16.21
Right now, I am overly focused on so much
I want to do it all, but it's too much
Career, path, branding
Health, school, kids and me
Money, family, pandemic

Fears, future telling, how to invest
Dreams...what if
My mind is filled with all of this

Its costing me time, emotions, clarity and peace
When I don't live in my truth, I feel like I am slowly
dying

I am burning out when I don't get enough sleep
When I don't follow my heart, when I say yes to
too many things

My core values help steer me
Health, honesty, family
Reflecting, writing, journaling
Being of value, always learning

Where is burning just too much these days?
Too much good, too much bad- too much in any
way
Too much yoga, not enough sleep
Too many meetings, not enough working out or
losing weight

Finding my purpose will help fill me up
Consistent income

Traveling and sleep
Those are all things I think I want/need

I need and want more sleep
More laughter, more money
More faith and less fear
Less mistrust, masks, force, bullying, agendas and
tears

I need/want more poetry
More exercise- I want that for me
More date night, or date days-just that time
More meatless meals and more time outside
Less scarcity mindset
Less questions and what ifs
More smiles, rest, beauty and clarity
More togetherness but less judgement and
rushing

I have made and am making peace with it
That you can die from covid

I think a person who cares about me would want
me to know
To write that book, go drive and focus on one
thing at a time to get it done

They would see me struggling with me wanting to
do it all
And tell me I don't have to be the perfect me, wife
and mom

I want to give myself permission to change
Permission to rest and take a break
Permission to be in the moment
Permission to succeed, grow and shine and be
great-and own it
Permission to outgrow and evolve
I have to come home to myself in order to start
So, starting today I will nap/rest
Starting today I will sing and listen to music
Starting today I will drink some shakeology
Starting today I will flow, write, maybe even drink
tea

Make the choice, yes or no
Just do it, and see where it goes

8.30.21
The summer I had hoped I would have, hasn't
been all I hoped for
It's been less, it's been more
We made it on a couple of trips

Some places, we didn't yet make it
We spent time with family
We created new memories
I even participated in mystics magic school
Thankful for scholarships, connections and the
time to
We made it to celebrations, birthday parties
Some with masks, some without-everyone has
different comforts and boundaries
For one of our children, we experienced summer
school
Not just that, but our first in-person school
We celebrated sober-versaries
My first pop up table with two books sold, meant
so much to me
We tried going back to church, in person
It wasn't for us, for different reasons
I completed open-source wellness program
I started coaching training, in a different way-yet
again
I took advantage of old gift cards
Had my first facial and enjoyed the healing
through the fears and scars

My heart needs me to make decisions

My mind needs me to sleep, rest and be in
reflections
My spirit needs me to get clear
To set my intentions and hold true, even in fear
To get outside- for any amount of time
To eat less meat, even if it's just me- my feeling is
only mine
To participate in more grounding
Meditate, yoga time, go bare feet

A yes, to me-feels like a smile
A real smile, like a child
A yes, feels like peace
Happiness, tears---release

A no, to me -feels like pressure
Feels like anxiety and stress- it feels like trouble

Right now, I am sitting with yoga membership in
question
I have found a home and community here, but
money is a distraction
I am feeling like I am in no place of long-term
commitment
Even though I know I want to be here long term- I
just am scared to bring disappointment

I wish I could let go of worry
Right now, I am cultivating- me
Right now, I am cultivating my purpose
My income, my peace- my choices

As summer is coming to an end
My soul needs- to begin again
My soul needs to not let go of "summer"
I have so much more I still want, so much more

I promise to care for me
To rest, to sleep
To give my all to what I have said yes to
To continue to align with me and all the moves I
choose into

9.22.21
I have put so much on my plate
I said I wouldn't but then I couldn't ...I had to walk
in faith
I have set myself up for challenges and growth
I have felt into when I say yes and when I say no
I have decided in-person school is not for the
majority of us

We have decided that together and it's good to
know that much
There are no more options of remote learning
where we live
So, we have to find online schools- in different
districts

I am learning about work-trades
I am learning that people see things in me- gifts I
can embrace

I keep saying yes when I feel it is in alignment
If I feel it brings me fear and opportunity to grow-I
am not saying no if it's in alignment
In alignment with who I am, who I want to be
Where I am, where I'm going
The connections and timing are divine- I couldn't
have predicted what's coming to be
Ambassador for freedomyoga, Va for courageous
life society
Journey to right livelihood
Life mastery, my life is filled with so much

Writing books is alive for me, right now
The Shaklee challenge is alive for me right now
Removing skin tags, getting braces

Going to Burney falls- meeting new faces
Learning to drive, wanting to coach
So much is alive for me- I want to do more than
hope
I want to know
And I do know
All of this is screaming in my soul
Opportunities for pop up tables
I am being pulled in many directions
But I am making the choices and decisions

10.6.21
I am in bed, I am tired
I am trying to flow and prioritize rest but my heart
wants to accomplish so much more

So much I want to do
But I'm still doing what I want to do

Pulled in so many directions, low energy
But I am allowing these pulls, I am giving that
energy
I am drained and exhausted
But all this is all I've wanted

The qualities I am bringing in

Are writing and reflection

Wonder, to me-
are all the places my imagination and higher self
can take me
it's what I see in my toddlers' eyes and hear in her
words
its in my children's hand drawn pictures

wonder, is in the pictures I take- both candid and
posed for
its in the minds I can't read but all that I can see
when I take the time to observe
wonder is so present in my life at this time
it is present as I write
as I set goals, as I fail
wonder never fails

wonder brings so many benefits
it brings perspective
it brings me courage
space to dream and try again

I feel like I need to wonder less
That I need to embody more and apply all that
wonder presents

10.6.21
Notice an object
Just observe it

I see a back pillow
Is it gray or blue?
Who tells us what we know?
What makes the truth true?

Wrinkles means its soft
I know its soft yet firm enough to support me the
way o need and want
Wrinkles mean, it can mold with me and doesn't
have to be just one way

10.6.21
I don't like the beach
I don't like the sand in my shoes or my clothes
I don't like to get wet, if it wasn't in my plans

But I have gone to the beach the last two Sundays
My 3-year-old loves the water and sand
I love seeing life through her
I love seeing her smile and wonder
It helps bring me happiness

It helps me take off my shoes
Get wet, why not- she asked me to

I love the air
I love the views
I love the idea of the beach
I love when the sand is hot, on my feet

I enjoy getting creative

We do things for others, we don't do for ourselves
But it is for me too....

10.6.21
I will bring in more wonder by blowing more
bubbles
Putting the phone down to play
Get outside daily because I love how it feels when
I do
And when I do, we do

11.10.21
There is ease
Ease does live in me
In my breathe and my mind
There's an ease in closing my eyes

Ease in my journey, I didn't say it was easy
Ease in my connections, I am so thankful for so
many opportunities
Ease in my reflections
Ease in where I am
Ease in gratitude
...not everyone will understand

If I think about it, I can feel what's opposite of
ease
The feeling in my ponytail, yeah, I feel that
differently
So, I will release
We don't have to sit with what isn't serving us
beautifully
We can change what doesn't feel right
So here is my invite

I invite you to look for ease
I invite you to feel your reality
Its all here and can be true
The good, the bad- the in-between too

I love when others manifestations come true
When hard things happen, I look for the gratitude

I wonder in hard times-what dreams and prayers
are being answered through
What manifestation is coming true

Recently we have had several ER visits
We got our first fur baby family member after
years of resistance
Our household got smaller and its now "just us"
So much is changing and in the unknown, I trust

I have taken pride in only one of us having to test
during this whole pandemic wellness journey
Recently our youngest had to, and it really hit me
But I was able to move through it with acceptance
I raised my questions
I was there to witness and record it all
I was there to document and support through the
hard

11.10.21
Less is more
But more is more -also

I am clearing out what no longer serves me
So, I can make space for all that does

Letting go is hard
But holding on feels frustrating

Less is more
Less stuff, more open space
Less hiding, more truth
Less struggle, more surrender

Less doesn't have to mean less (good)
Every no, is a yes
And every yes, a no

More is more
When is more, more?
I am trying to be less of a hoarder
I am trying to outgrow scarcity mindset

I am inviting in more fun
More faith, more alignment

More gratitude is never too much, for me
I'd love more music, and the time to be free
Free to dance, to listen and sing out loud
More music please, to help me ground

More is more

It can be negative or positive
Depending where you place your attention

What do I want less of?
What do I want more of?

The darkness of this season doesn't upset me
I don't enjoy it being darker earlier, feeling like its
limiting me
Cold makes me fear of getting sick
I have kids, I want wellness

I would like to cultivate more light
More gardening, more plants-inside and outside
I would like to cultivate more money
More published books—all the energy it brings
I would like to cultivate more dream come trues
It would allow me to have less fears, less stress,
less worry too

If I had less "should"
I would have more flow

11.24.21
I am filled with grief and gratitude
Grief of the life before all these rules

Grief of life before this kind of separation
Gratitude for life and all its lessons
Gratitude for choice and change
Gratitude to choose and make peace with others
doing the same

12.1.21
Let your fear go
Let me be guided by my fear, its here to help me
hear my soul
Let the time flow
Let us know, all the things we know

Make me whole again
Make my scarcity mindset heal into what it isn't

12.1.21
I don't want to yell at the kids or raise my voice
I don't want to get sick or not have a choice
I don't want to be bullied or forced into anything
I don't want to gamble with life or time or energy

I don't want to beat myself up or hold myself back
I don't want to feel lack

I don't want to over-eat

I don't want to be too busy

I don't want clutter or useless stuff
I want to use what I have, or let it go- enough is
enough

What if, all is as it should be
What if, everything I don't want-doesn't have to
be
What if, it already isn't
What if, time is timeless
What if

12.1.21
Permission granted, to write and travel and be
true to me
I know I want to own a home, move away and be
with lots of family
I want to feel at home
To feel safe, heard, supported and ok to not have
control

I am devoted to my dreams
I am devoted to me
I am devoted to change

I am devoted to a "better" life and nothing getting in the way

I am so thankful for this group of women who have made it into my heart. I am thankful to have Barb Klein as a coach. I am thankful for the prompts, meditation, reflections, break-out rooms, check in-s, check-outs, journaling time, music and everything else.

How can you care for your soul today? (This week?)

_____

_____

_____

_____

_____

_____

_____

_____

_____

_____

_____

QUEST

The mothers quest manifesto challenge is a free 7-day challenge.
Followed by the spark your epic life summer series (I was grandfathered in) but decided to invest anyways because I wanted to help someone else who can't afford it, because People have done this for me.

Lena Ayala-Velasquez
September 23, 2020 ·
Shared with Your friends and friends of anyone tagged

I always love this question.
what are you on a quest for right now?
thank you Julie Lieberman Neale
right now ......
I am most on a quest for living epic, living out loud "living everyday like it's my birthday". putting in

the work and faith (because fear is real) to do the things I have been longing to do

living like it's my birthday every day: October is our celebration month because of all the birthdays (mine and the two oldest kids included) just getting what you want/need, asking for it and feeling like you can splurge for it.... doing things that are fun and on the dream lists, (knowing these ways of being don't have to be just 1 time a year or for holidays)

for me living epic and out loud and like it's my birthday right now looks like:

*I am seeing a chiropractor: Dr. Heidi Wroebel

*I am doing workouts with beachbod and Lynda Zepeta Gutierrez

*I am in coaching groups(courageous life society with Jessica Stung)

mothers quest milestone hike with Julie

I am in soul care with Barb Klein

I have joined mama medicine with Beth Sachnoff

*I have signed up for tiny book course to write book #1-for me and I get to do it with mothersquest community

*I have done virtual assistance with two people I admire this year

*The kids are having school from home. 1 child has made it into remote learning and the other two are still in flexible learning. while the baby is enjoying preschool from home with us

*I am learning, I am growing, I am changing, I am changing my stories and living the ones I wish to see true

I continue to meet new people and grow and have new opportunities and I am challenging myself to expand my comfort zones

I have enjoyed overcoming overwhelm with Jennifer White which is starting up again soon

I have enjoyed the pop up healing center and gratitude challenge with Adelina Tancioco and being a part of the surrendered healing community and events

I have joined the mommymillionair community with the free challenge they offered earlier

I have been following Micki Morris and will soon do more with her, I can feel it

there's just so much I have been blessed to do over the years, this year, during COVID and am currently working on

but everything starts with you, with you saying YES

with investing in yourself

with asking about scholarships and asking for
what you need, having support
Faith over fear
Flowing not forcing

3.20.20
I choose gratitude, because- its grounding
I already know, I can do hard things
But that doesn't mean its easy to do hard things
So much is on my mind- addiction, moving and
coparenting
My journals will be my pandemic scrapbook
I want to document all that I can so one day I can
look back, almost like a time capsule

So much is on my heart that I want to embody
Music, school, yoga, meditation, prayer and
storytelling

I am trying to take away the struggle that doesn't
need to be here
I am trying not to consume too much of anything
that isn't serving me, I am starting there
And that is a lot to start with
That is a lot to practice

3.23.20

Gratitude comes to me with ease
I don't often explain my why-I am practicing

I am thankful that with our move, it means my
husband works closer to home
It makes me feels safer and worry less- to know
To know he doesn't have to wake up as early as
he used to
To know he won't get home as late as he used to
To know, now we can take advantage of lunch
together
To know now, it will be overall healthier and
happier

I am thankful for my family
Who live upstairs, in the back, in this home and
across the street
I feel so protected and supported
I feel helpful and so much happiness

I am thankful to be home with my kids
I know not everyone can do this
It is rare and I am soaking it in
Who knows when this time will be a memory of
moments.

Today I will get the baby to sleep earlier for nap
I will step outside, with or without the kids
Today I will not tell my children to wait
I will say yes and see it creates
Today I will take care of me
My house, and my community
 I will do this by staying home
Praying and offering my support

4.30.20
7 weeks later, it's not perfect but we are ok
I am made to be your teacher-I have been since
born day
Moment by moment, we will create new plans as
we need to
Life is happening as it is meant to

My body is telling me to listen
To go outside and connect to earth again
To get away from the screens
To rest to sleep

Mentally, I already know-what my body needs
I just need to listen because I haven't been
applying

I am re-norming
I give myself permission to be allowed to want
things
I am not my past anymore
I am grateful, even for the concerns
I want a healthier relationship with technology
I want to be a coach; I know it's already me

Tomorrow I am giving up my phone
Taking a break from social media, because it's
been calling at me to do so

I am constantly charging my phone
I am already thinking about how in missing 4 days,
how then will I catch up with the world
I enjoying learning, sharing information and
connecting with others
I love being open and honest, having
documentation that's mine forever
I love Facebook memories
They mean so much to me
I love meeting new people, especially now
But I know I need to do this right now

My hands, eyes and brain all hurt

I need a break for sure
I need to lead by example for my kids
When the phone is down, what will then be the distraction?

4.30.20
7 weeks later, it's not perfect but we are ok
I am made to be your teacher-I have been since born day
Moment by moment, we will create new plans as we need to
Life is happening as it is meant to

My body is telling me to listen
To go outside and connect to earth again
To get away from the screens
To rest to sleep

Mentally, I already know-what my body needs
I just need to listen because I haven't been applying

I am re-norming
I give myself permission to be allowed to want things
I am not my past anymore

I am grateful, even for the concerns
I want a healthier relationship with technology
I want to be a coach; I know it's already me

Tomorrow I am giving up my phone
Taking a break from social media, because it's
been calling at me to do so

I am constantly charging my phone
I am already thinking about how in missing 4 days,
how then will I catch up with the world
I enjoying learning, sharing information and
connecting with others
I love being open and honest, having
documentation that's mine forever
I love Facebook memories
They mean so much to me
I love meeting new people, especially now
But I know I need to do this right now

My hands, eyes and brain all hurt
I need a break for sure
I need to lead by example for my kids
When the phone is down, what will then be the
distraction?

4.30.20
Its not always easy to do
But I hope you find the courage to put yourself
first

Treat yourself as good as you do others

Listen to your body
Hear it and take action

Get support, ask for help

Say yes, say no
Do what serves you
Let go of anything that doesn't
And always be thankful

Count your blessing sand face your challenges
with patience
Its ok to be real, to be transparent

Feel it all and then move on
Saying goodbye to April before I get off Facebook
and only journal

5.1.20
Day 1, no social media

I open my eyes to a text from my mom, its
important
I call, but it's not too important
I want to scroll through Facebook while on the
phone
Last night I deleted 7 apps off of my phone
I still have way too many apps on my phone
But I am trying to make it less tempting, in hopes I
won't want to get on

Last night I wanted to post
But why do I want/need to post?

I have a list of things I would like to do today
I feel like I have more time to have time today

Today I had a great belly laugh with my cousin in
the car
When is the last time I have laughed that hard?
Today in the mail, was a letter from me to me
What perfect timing

So much wasn't going right this morning

This day was my day to get it right but it wasn't
happening
I am ok with it not going as I hoped
I am thankful for all that is accomplished and for
all that isn't going wrong

My cousin tried showing me a meme but I had to
look away
I told her I am taking a social media break
My daughter said people are going to worry not
seeing me posting
My brother said I won't last 4 days-this says so
much obviously

On our bike ride today, I didn't take my phone
I took my camera instead, like old times

I have gone to my phone several times to press
the fb app without realizing
Then I remember "oh yea" its not there for me
I have wanted to post about my day so many
times today
Why do I want to post about my day?

5.1.20
We got a letter about the options for school next
year
So many are worried for the second wave of
cases, I too have fears

I am thankful today my sons throat doesn't hurt
I am thankful for all we made it to experience
before this pandemic took over
I am sad for the places we didn't make it to
Who knows what options will be like when all of
this is through?

Stores and places are looking so different
With stickers where to stand, faces with masks
and big plastic dividers you can see through but is
for protection

We have made it through pandemics before
Maybe now, jobs will care more
They will care more when their employees are sick
They will care less about money and more about
wellness

How is this real life?

5.2.20

The baby was up at 3 in the morning unable to
sleep
So, that means- I was unable to sleep
So many things cross my mind
Like why am I up at this time?
Is there a bigger picture for a reason why?
The "to do" list is on my mind
Is the baby getting sick?
She doesn't feel warm, did she have a bad dream
or something?
I can't get comfy with another child at the foot of
the bed
I had a dream about my grandpa-we didn't speak, I
couldn't talk to him
All I could do was watch and listen
I wanted to interact but I guess this dream had a
different message

Today we got $5 masks from a friend
I love to support good people's businesses
I love the quality, I love the look
They are re-usable
I want to publicly post and thank her and advertise
for her
But I am taking a break from social media

I tell others in case they want to by some
Word of mouth still is good

I want to post about my dream
I don't need to keep checking amazon tracking, so
why do I feel the need?

Homeschool, nature school, forest school and
unschooling
What will graduations next month look like, will
they even be happening

People are messaging me on social media, texting
me why am I not answering
My husband is trying to show me stuff but
I'm not looking
He says he will get off his phone to hang out
He is very supportive and happy with my timeout

I wanted to help advertise my brothers' new
beanies
He sold out almost immediately
We watched movie
I even got to bed early and no need for cbd

5.3.20
Today is Sunday, day 3 of no social media
Less phone, less tv

How do I post more meaningful once I am back on?
I want to still be me, but I want to have more intention
Open, honest, transparent with the good and bad
That is just me, I need that
Facebook is my diary and my photo album
People connect with others through me, people come to me for my words and albums
People message me inspired when I am not trying to be
I know my words matter-whether I am or am not told directly

Today cousins joined our bike ride
The streets are crowded with people walking, biking and driving by.
We even saw family friends biking
We all kept distance but of course did some chatting.
So nice to see people we know, people we enjoy

Someone I could text and not need social media
for to connect with.
My in-laws came over and we all played board
games
Today is our daughter's best friend's birthday.
So, my husband made them a pizza for their family
They gave us masks, the kids hugged and spent
time opening gifts and taking pictures.
People we care about lost loved ones to c19
Every crowded street makes me feel like now is
the time to say in and away from reality.

My husband says he misses reading my long posts
about our days
He misses reading my gratitude's...I would've
never known he felt that way.
We know people who work in hospitals
One has 5 cases at San Leandro hospital.
So that is a bit scary
But what isn't these days or life before c19.

I am thankful for every moment.

5.4.20
Day 4 no social media, less phone, less tv

Today I dyed my hair and did my daughters tips
Family stopped by for hugs and these pandemic
rules are always changing.
My son was able to go for a bike ride with friends
They didn't need masks because of exercise and
distance.
On our bike ride, Athena was singing
Then I played music from my phone-we all joined
the singing.
People smiled at us as we went by
The kids are taking me by surprise.
Our oldest chose a fade and jeans today
He never chooses those things, what a day.

I put apps back on my phone today with
excitement
No urge to rush back on but excited to have the
option.

I did get on ig this morning
I did do some scrolling.
I'll never catch up on the past 4-5 days
My eyes are starting to hurt, back to a break.

5.5.20
I want to be inspired

I want to inspire
I want to feel in the know
But not with too much at once, always -all the
time- you know?
I want social media to serve me
When it doesn't, I need to get off- that's what I
need
I don't want it to take away from my family, my
goals and life
I don't want it to drain me this time

5.11.20
I have had a headache all day
So, I haven't really been on social media today
But then I hopped on and saw Julie live
As I listened, I could feel the pain subside
As I journaled-my headache would stop
But when the video ended, I feel the tension
coming back strong

I told my husband, usually answers come so easy
But today I have been avoiding
Avoiding the reflection question
But something I wrote stood out as very
important

"Coach and teach others"
This is my calling; it has been and I left it
unanswered
I have felt this all my life but especially when CEC
closed
During mentor masterclass with Jeanine yoder
Its hard to claim this because I have been avoiding
this calling for 3 years
And now, no other smaller callings feel present or
matter the way these matters.

Writing books, being a life coach of some kind-is
my calling
What if I claim it and it goes nowhere? What will
that say about me?
What if I claim this and am still not ready?
How can I claim this when I am still unsure of all
that will follow for me?

My gratitude for all mentors/coaches and
teachers, has always led me here
Do my challenges and imperfections mean I can't
be a coach, especially one with fears?
The fact that I look to others for coaching, does
that mean I can't be a coach?
How do I know all I don't?

Hearing others speak and be
I always think I live and breathe these practices
and reality
I am always helping others
I love to serve others
I love writing about the good, the bad-the real
I love being transparent with how I feel
I live by gratitude
I love learning

So, what am I scared of?
Why am I so emotional?

I have to let my feelings feel
I have to feel all that is real
I am all about integrity and reflection
I am all about documentation

How can I be different? Unique?
Can I just know, that will come with being me?

"I am not hiding, I am healing"
Julie suggests I call in y ancestors after declaring

I am carolina Madeleine-Guadalupe Ayala-
Velasquez. I am daughter of Chantal Madeleine
Giordano. I am granddaughter of madeleine
Giordano, lupe padilla and katie padilla.

5.12.20
I have family visiting
Much needed human connection with family
I love the kids playing
I love adult connecting

I carved time for me to join this live- for me
I am so thankful for Julie

5.12.20
What is essential to me, is protecting my peace
Trusting my intuition and faith-let that guide me
Following my heart
Getting outside, alone and together
Being in the moments and having gratitude
through it all
Allowing myself to pause
"Have to's" that can wait
Like house chores, shopping, unpacking and also
knowing I want to create space

Knowing I want to create the environment I truly vision is important to me
Little by little I am getting that done
I am allowing it to happen rather than force it to become

5.15.20
My name is carolina ayala-velasquez. I believe in being transparent with the good and bad. That gratitude grounds us and helps us move through all situations. I believe wea are all lifelong learners and as a coach we are learning from each other. I believe in reflection and documentation.

I stand for leading by example and those practices can be used for all ages.

I manifest.

I even see me writing those books I have always seen myself doing. And, maybe that comes first to help me become the coach I want to be... cheers to figuring it all out. Or letting it all happen without "figuring it out."

Who am I?

I am a write, a teacher, a mother, a photographer, a care-taker, a healer, a poet, a wife. I am thoughtful and honest.

I am on a quest for making changes. To creating the environment that brings me peace. I am on a quest to treat myself with the same love, care and support that I give to others. I am on a quest to level up. Mom and teacher will always be me, but now- the title of coach. I have been a coach before, but now to level up. Life coach and to define what that would look like for me. I am on a quest often. Finding me constantly.

I am on a quest for change. Intentional and actual.

Time to make that happen

5.15.20
There is so much to me that I want to explore
Like making t-shirts and being a party planner
Creating dessert tables and starting a podcast
Writing books and becoming more holistic
To get more educated on substance abuse
And start a blog, too

5.16.20

When I find something that makes me a better me, adds value to myself and my life and my light- I want to share that with those I love. I want to share with those I feel it may help.

I want to live in a world where we all know and have access to support that helps us become our best self.

I believe we can all make the world a better place, if we start with ourselves first.

Here is what I know for sure, that it is easy to not love ourselves the way that we love others.

Gratitude has always been what ground me, keeps me driven and dreaming and believing in something more. Especially during the hard times. But gratitude does not mean we have to stay comfortable in what is. I no longer believe that just because I can always find the good, that- that has to be good enough.

We are all lifelong learners. We all have our own journey. No one is alone, we learn that through showing up and realizing we have great support systems when we build community and relationships.

I believe the "bad" parts of life, are just as good as the "good" parts and I am on a quest to help others trust and believe in not only that but who they are.
Who you are, is who the world needs.

5.16.20
Why am I more comfortable behind the scenes?
I am not always happiest there.
Work is not always noticed or appreciated.
It's a way to hide.
To not have accountability.
I have no problem helping promote others.
But when it comes to work, teaching, parenting and me- I am more of a behind the scenes.

I am 100% committed to investing in myself.
Joining mothersquest spark your epic life group coaching series.

I care about this because I am on a quest for
finding myself and helping serve others.
I will do this by signing up and paying.

5.16.20
Looking back, I have always kept pictures
around/memories
They are like positive quotes/moments in time for
me

I always kept a journal, for my memories
For my growth-of my journey

Documentation of my life, our lives, our world-
through my lens

I always made "vision boards" with pictures,
quotes, art and statements.

Looking back, I am like my parents without even
knowing or trying to be.
Much I learned what I do and don't want to be.
My mom celebrated birthdays, inviting all
My mom took pictures of the good and
embarrassing moments
My mom kept pets

My mom asked for help
My mom kept a full house

5.17.20
To coach someone else means I have to have it all
together. That's the negative story I tell myself.
But I don't have to have it all together. And that is
why I can and should do this.

5.17.20
I am working on me
I invited someone else, as an individual-aside from
our titles of who we "need to be"
It adds an extra level to all of this experience
I wonder if we could be ourselves and honest
Not as coparents or past enemies
Just as two women, two human beings

My future self-vision didn't involve preschool
teaching last year
I am claiming and reclaiming me
I am finding me
Who I am in this world
Its emotional...but I keep hearing life coach.
Its who I am, it's my calling.
It's always been in front of me.

5.20.20

Right now, I am most on a quest for finding who I am and helping serve others.

I am so thankful to you Julie. For all of the times you sponsored me and to be grandfathered in to this experience. I offer this amount, for the future or this time around- so that it can pay for someone who can't afford the opportunity. Much like the situation I have been in so often. I am thankful to be able.

5.24.20

Mothers quest spark your epic life coaching series, this is my third time joining.

20 years from now, how old am I?
I see me now, but then in the future
Not older but wiser
Peaceful and happy

Space, big outdoors
Family, friends near by but not too close
There's a creek
A dog barking

Feels like "wake up" it's not real
Inside the house is peaceful
No clutter, so much space
Clean, calm, fresh air and tea

What do I need to know to get from where I am to
where you are?

You've always known what will help, you need to
let go
No mask, no pandemic

5.30.20
Yesterday I realized my moms' best friends, also
share kids. I now realize my mom was making
blended families work before I even knew details.
I wonder if she knew.
It's time to ask.

6.8.20
So much I want to do
Pinpointing something is hard
I want to be purposeful
I want o write books, start a podcast, start
coaching and embrace this virtual assisting that
people see in me

I want to donate, I want to volunteer
I am getting coached, working on myself-its
continual self-care
I am making body movement a habit
Trying to create intentional exercise
There's so much I want to teach my kids
I have visions for how we show up in the world

I have a struggle with screens
I love that in this community we can agree to
disagree
We don't have to agree in order to co-exist
I know that anyone who is involved with Julie has
good intent
I struggle with my relationship with social media

6.14.20
I am celebrating getting outdoors
I am celebrating intentional body movement
I am still working on creating the space I love (feel
and look) inside of my home
I have been cleaning, decluttering, organizing,
planting and its starting to look beautiful
I want to love my home, inside and out
I want to feel like I am home
I want to show it off if I want

Minimizing, getting new- I am creating a vision
I know space, closets and storage will make me
happy

I am thinking of my future home
My dream home

Of natural lights, gates/fences/safety,
Bricks on the outside, solar panels,
Guest space, yards, garden, fruit trees, parking,
garage basement for game nights and fun

I am big on intentional exercise, because it helps
me feel grounded, improves my sleep and energy,
makes me feel healthier and more beautiful, helps
my immune system

6.14.20
I have discovered that although I have identified
and claimed parts of me- I still need to take care
of other things first. Like self-care and wanting to
love my home environment. I need to invest in
things that will improve my life and let go of what
is no longer serving me.
I need to let go.

I need to stop trying to please everyone.
Stop holding everyone's emotions.
This experience was challenging and easy.
I have run into judgement, technical issues more
than once, twice I did this meeting from my
mother-in-law's home and borrowed a computer.
I gave back and paid although I didn't have to.
A coparent only joined the first session.
I have been open and honest.
I talked in the group online, did the peer
accountability buddies.

I am brave, I am open, I am honest, I am human.

6.30.20
My story of the day
Is to trust in the trust
Take action that matters
Time for change is time for truth, therapy
Trust in my timing
Teach and be teachable
Talk it, walk it
Treat myself
Take care of me and us
Try something new

10.27.20

What is present, writing my first tiny book, family time and rest

What if we did- go home and visit GOD can I be selfish or does that mean I am not worthy of such an option?
Id love to go see my loved ones in heaven
Id love to see GOD- for a visit, I feel like I have to be specific
I am not ready to die
Maybe a visit can wait, wait until my time
What goes GOD want me to know
I close my eyes, I pray and let go
Sometimes my children give me messages
I know they are heaven sent, I never question it
I breathe, I cry, I smile
I hold me for awhile

It doesn't have to be the perfect ending
That's the prompt I needed to start my beginning

What if we did – go home and visit GOD
What if we knew, we did not have to visit- to be with GOD?

When I stop to. think
When I stop to, see

I am well aware GOD is always here with me

This book I am working on is to help heal me and others
It's a message from GOD, from my dad

2020

There are things I am not willing to do for money
There are things I could lose
Money makes me feel safe
Money shows up for me when I need it
Money matters to me, it means I can give my loved ones a life to love
I believe money makes things happen
I make money that feels good
I realize I need to heal my money story and I am working on creating a different relationship with it

It is important to me that I earn more money to create a different life experience for me than I grew up in
It is important to me to save, for when I need or want it

It is important to me that I give back, help those in
need
People have done that for me
It is important I pay debts so that I don't have any
I am not even sure what's best for building credit
scores but I cannot stand owing money
I pay it off quickly
I don't like to owe,
So, I don't borrow

Healing is forever and on going
There will always be more work to do and learning
I have dreams that will cost me
I have dreams of a life that isn't based on money

2/23/21
I am feeling tired and a bit frustrated but also
happy to be here
Spark your epic life, is finally here
I am a mom to 4 and all are in different levels of
schooling
With my title and role, I feel I always have to be
specific about some things
Like the fact I am a stepmom,
A coparent, a second mom

I want so much for my children
I want no masks, better health, exercise and
socialization
I want outside time and less screens
I want some "normalcy" whatever that means
I want them to have more family time
Less regret and moments "ruined" or un-had times

I am asking myself what it would fully look like to
embrace this year
This year I want to help and serve others
In a bird's eye view I see a map
I see success down the road that's long, curvy
greatness through it all

The seeds I would plant would be a tree of my
books

5.4.21
I am curious about some things on my mind
What does it take to become worthy, to be on
someone's podcast and take up time?
What does it take to become an ambassador for a
month?
What does it take for people to want to know
you? To listen up?

5.16.21

If you ask me, what do I love, the answer comes
quickly
My children, my husband, my friends and family

Outside of them, what do I love?
I love writing, and reflecting, teaching and being in
the sun

I am on a quest for finishing
Keeping my momentum going
Doing what makes me happy
Living in my truth, honestly

Living in my truth means embracing the struggle
and happiness
It means sharing all of it

I have been ignoring whispers of going back to
school
Fear of math, knowing I need it to get to where I
want to
Fear of failing, so I don't even start
Fear of bad grades, what it would mean to get
them if I try hard

Fear of wasting money
Fear of not having enough to even start and get
this all going

Writing children's books, fear of the unknowns
How to get an illustrator, why can't my family get
the job done
What it means to get the person I dream of to
work with me
What if they say no, how can this happen
financially?
...and yet, I can see my future books on shelfs in
stores when I close my eyes
I can see this really going somewhere, I feel it
inside

Wanting to know how to drive, I want to help
Fear of crashing, hurting me -or even worse,
someone else
Fear of owing money I don't even have
Fear of ruining a car, that isn't paid off yet

I am wanting to teach
But I don't want the vaccine

I am feeling stuck with keeping momentum

I still want to be a coach
I still want to be an author of more books
I still want to teach
I want to be more present with my kids

So many moments have changed my life
So much is calling me
I want to own a house
I want more money
 I want to work for me

They aren't whispers anymore
I have named them
I have made steps but not yet completed

5.16.21
I won a free 45-minute consultation with the
handmade life/Katie
How does life know exactly what to give to me?
I am all about learning
I am all about evolving
And this win comes with face cream
I don't really use those things
But I am learning to take care of me
And natural is the way to get me to try new things

5.31.21
I am tired
I am feeling unaccomplished, even though I know
that thought makes me a liar
I know the truth
But I still feel how I do
Fears of the future- so many things on my mind
Lawyers, money, work, shots, masks, school and
time
I am feeling a bit overwhelmed with goals, dreams
and reality
I need to make time for sleep
Real sleep
Rest, for me

7.7.21
Times I felt wonder and surprise is when I think of
my inner child, picking up my kids toys and
remembering me at their age, publishing my book,
missing being a preschool teacher, being a
mom/teacher,

Earlier I yelled/raised my voice
Then I had to remember to breathe

"Oh, she must have been having fun making a mess"
I had to reframe my thoughts and feelings

The book journey is constant wonder and surprise

I miss teaching and being paid to do what I love
Mom me, not working- I have to remind myself to still play

Our children are perfect, as is
So are we
So are our parents...

MYSTICS

I was introduced to the mystics society thanks to Julie of MothersQuest. I have been able to participate in several of the courses and opportunities that Lindsay Pera of the mystic's society offers. I am a member of the mystics society, I was able to join mystics magic school thanks to a scholarship available and I was gifted a space in Journey To Right Livelihood.
My shared reflections are just a few of many. They do not share my whole experience of the group; they do not speak for the courses or

179

person in charge. They are simply a few
reflections that came to me during a certain time
of life thanks to whatever setting I was in.

12.21.20
Renewal of creative path

What showed up this year? What came?
For me, so much. Change, growth, opportunity,
surrender, abundance, travel, sobriety, dream
come trues

What came, that felt like magic?
Chiropractor(s), church is here, moving back to
alameda, school at home

Title for the past year would be?
Manifestation. Surrender. Delivered. Zen. Fulfilled.
Soul-care. Dream come true. 2020 vision.

How can you experience the unexpected magic?
I flowed
Flowing not forcing
Faith over fear
My goal was zen
Learn to dream again

What title might you assign the year ahead?
Intentional

6.8.21
What's your magic story?
I grew up believing my mind creates reality.
Charmed show, magic books and gems. When
others said it was evil or against religion
But the magic stayed all around
Powerful, very real
As I continue to find "my people" it's all coming
back but welcomed and encouraged

I have visioned many things that came true. Good
and bad.
Sickness, moving back, each of my kids, writing
self-publishing, being a teacher, empathy,
intuition, vibes, trust
Dreams

When I think of wands, I think of: my toothbrush,
spatula, mop, broom, sage, sticks, candle, pen,
pencil, camera holder

When I think of spells and potions, I think of:
bubble baths and bath bombs, poetry, lotions,
prayer, journaling, face masks, tea, essential oils,
reflecting, music, food

6.22.21
What is something showing up in your life that
you want more of?
Money, plants, clarity, healthy food and drinks,
space, beauty

What is something showing up that you do not
want more of?
School stress, clutter, masks, pressure of what to
do

What would you like to manifest?
Career, purpose, money
Home
Travel, family, health, safety
Trust, faith, stand strong in power

What is something now/present that you treasure
deeply?
My family, my book, my journals, my pictures,
groups I am in, travel, cameras

6.29.21

I picked my own poetry book to pull from today
What wants to be seen, what should I know about?
I want to know about my purpose/career, money, home, traveling, family, health, faith, school and trust.
But to be specific I want to know am I meant to wrote more books? Is authorship for me?
I turn to page 67 in my book, its day 7(my dad's favorite number) iris is only 7 here with questions of her own.
I think of young me at 7.
When I die is on my mind
It's been a good year but it just started
Only had dad 21 days into new year
What if I only have 21 days to live left?
What do I believe?
It's crazy the question I asked, because what's really on my mind last night's thoughts and what's on my heart has been death

How will my kids remember me?
How can I help create that now?

Fear and courage

The page I got was the answer to the questions I
didn't ask about, last night's thoughts

Do I have time to live out my purpose and calling?

Feeling emotional and heavy

I know I am meant to write more books and do
more with life
I knew the answers to the question I started with

8.23.20
What is life asking of me right now?
Right now, it asking me to share myself, to put me
out there, to become me, to step into me

Inclusive life Accelerator:
Thanks to an available scholarship and thanks to
Julie inviting me. I was able to attend Anti-racism
with mothersquest and Nicole lee. I was also able
to join the accelerator. My reflections and shares
are just a few that came to me. My reflections do
not represent these groups or anyone other than
myself.

6.17.21
Day 1.
We were asked what is exhaustion here to teach us?
For me it's here to teach me how to rest, when to rest. It is here to teach me how to recharge. To come home back to me and let that be more than enough. To feel more alive. The importance of sleep.

I am laying down the imposter syndrome. I heard the calling, the scholarship that was available and I took action so that I could be here. Not knowing what to expect, but knowing I wanted to be in it. It is my first time here.

I am bringing myself to share. I bring my honesty, an open mind, gratitude and emotions.

I hope to get connections from this. I hope to meet new people and build community. I want to grow into who I am and meant to be. And I love to learn new things.

My word for 2020 is: finally. Faith. Flow. Embrace. Rest.
And in 2021: dig deeper

I can be present and busy in work but not feel alive. More like a zombie. I feel more alive when I am laying in yoga in final rest- being present with myself.

I shouldn't have to have excuses or reasons. I want my kids in remote learning. That should be good enough.

In 2020 I embraced my knowledge, power, voice, dreams, faith, reality, support, intuition, resources, my truth, my mind, my callings, my space and myself.

To me, so far – covid has taught us a lot
-That kids can learn from home
-People can work from home, save gas, be with family, take off when they are sick. People can be valued for who they are and what they bring to the table. They are more than just a body to fill the space or a need to be met. They matter
-shots are free, they can be

-teachers and immigrants are essential and always have been
-essential people are still expendable
-cures can be made
-the world can stop
For any cause
-curfews can be placed and upheld
Bars can close earlier and for good
Homeless can be helped...and also aren't being taken care of enough
-doctor visits aren't so necessary and can be done virtually
-notes from doctors for school aren't so important
-janitors are essential
-people deserve more pay and less hustle
-food banks save lives
-online shopping is easy
-opportunity for anyone to create their own businesses is possible
-elders can shop earlier than the rest
-virtually, so much can get done
-unemployment is available for many
-entrepreneurs make money
-police brutality and protests don't stop
-breaks, rest and pausing is so important for our well being

-garden at home

Being afraid pushes me- I like a challenge. Being afraid freezes me at times, then I don't move forward.
Being hopeful and optimistic is me. This feels most edgy. Because you have to face fears and create change by taking action and facing hurt.
In my body it makes me feel anxious and overwhelmed.

6.18.21

People knew I was beyond my time- before I understood.
But, as I get back to me, I see I was on my right path long ago and I am being guided back (to me.)
I am reminded and restored.
I don't feel urgency, I feel I've been coming into it for a while.

In these different groups I don't see age, time or differences. I just see relationships, relatable and just being.

To get here, to be here- stuff has shifted for me.

I am privileged to be here; in the sense I knew
how to make the most of a scholarship spot. I had
people guide me.
How can I help others get here?

I have been taught and am learning, we are all on
time. Whether age 30 or 60. And then I have a
piece of me that says "how do we get to this place
sooner?" and help others realize it, now.

"It's not which thing is true, its- both things are
true!"
My daughter is 3 and potty training. She is on her
time. And mine. The support.
Right now, I am helping create my child's inner
child
Through experiences, trauma and life.

My inner child wants me to know, she never left
She needs me, to come back and let her in
I want to tell child me....

What dreams have you made real in your life-time, so far?

_____

_____

_____

_____

_____

_____

_____

_____

_____

_____

FREEDOM

Lena Ayala-Velasquez
July 26 · 21
Shared with Your friends

Freedom Yoga has been in my life since February 2021. I was in a point in my life where I had wanted to make yoga a practice in my living, for a long time. I had been doing some yoga on my own through videos, but I was not making it a daily practice the way I wanted to.

Thanks to surrendered Healing's gratitude challenge, I won a month of unlimited yoga from Freedom Yoga. This was a big motivation to really give yoga a chance. I had nothing to lose and everything to gain. By the end of my free unlimited month, I also won second place in making it to my mat most that month.

After meeting with Kim through zoom, I knew I was in the right place. She made time to connect with me, to ask about me as a person and to share what freedom yoga was about. Kim is so generous with her gifts, her time, her attention, and her teaching. She is more than a leader, the space she has created has built such a beautiful community.

We are now at the end of July, and I have been a paying member ever since March. I have zero regrets. Yoga has become an almost daily practice for me. I am someone who has suffered from chronic back pain for over a decade and yoga has helped me stretch, breathe, cope, and restore.

Here in Freedom Yoga, I feel like I have found another family for myself and my family. My kids and husband have joined yoga classes. My family has seen the difference in me, in my health and attitude.

Yoga is one piece of what it takes for me to be a better me, but it is what I look forward to in the morning to start my day feeling empowered, grounded, and accomplished. I constantly feel challenged, and I constantly feel proud.

I have tried to attend almost every class and teaching experience. I am constantly amazed at how every teacher is different and yet everything flows. I love the themes of the month; I love the variety of classes to choose from. I love that so many options of class times allow me capacity to attend, while also living the inconsistent day to day life that has been due to the pandemic.

I feel welcome, I feel supported, I feel like I am where I am meant to be.
thank you Kim and everyone in Freedom Yoga Union City. All of the teachers, all of the families, pets, and opportunities.

Lena Ayala-Velasquez
September 19 · 21
Shared with Your friends

I am proud to say all these months later I am an "ambassador" for freedom yoga.

I now even have a promo code

I will tell you why I love freedom yoga and why paying the monthly fee has been worth it to me.

I experience a lot of back pain; I have since having my almost 14-year-old.

Last year I started seeing a chiropractor and it really helped me.

Before I was seeing a chiropractor, I had tried yoga and couldn't make it through the pain, my mindset wasn't able to shift to something better and the tears were in my eyes.

Then life started coming together as I made changes in my life.

I came to moment of needing to pause with my chiropractor. (Who I would see at least a few times a month) but at almost $90 a visit, to me it made more sense to invest that almost same price to monthly yoga.

I love starting my morning with yoga. Although my children are home, I have found space enough for my mat and me to be.

My kids even join me at times, even my husband.

Yoga continues to be a challenge for me. Everywhere from the mindfulness, the breathing, the commitment and the poses.

It has also become a part of my lifestyle. When I go without it, my family notices differences in me- in my mood and how I feel.

I notice the differences in me when I do and don't show up.

It wasn't easy to "not quit", it was hard. In the beginning it felt like a workout. Sometimes I still feel like I "should" know more by now and be "better" at this practice "by now" but, I am human.

It's a constant practice. A practice I enjoy. I am stronger, I feel stronger. I feel more at peace. I feel happier.

I have met so many wonderful souls. I love this community and new chosen family.

I am so thankful for this journey. I am so excited for my growth in this space and time.

This has enhanced my life in many ways.

I know this is a long post.

But if you have ever felt moved or called or interested in yoga and this sounds good to you...please join.

I am not saying you will have the same experience as me.

Yoga is something I have wanted in my life for a long time. I have no doubts that it has worked out for me because I am at a point in my life where alignment and everything was right. I found the way to pay, without a "job" and with bills.

I didn't know I could get so much from yoga, virtually. But it has been such a good time. I learn so much about myself every time I show up to my mat...even when I don't.

I have won two "who can make it to your mat the most" challenges. Sometimes I took class 3 times a day.

I don't make it every single day.

Sometimes all I do is "make it"

but I always get something out of my experience.

Lena Ayala-Velasquez
July 9 · 21
Shared with Your friends

This morning after yoga class we were asked, what do you want to take from your mat?

I said I want to take the courage. I was on camera today, even with it being recorded. For me it's a challenge to be on camera in general. Because I see myself and I don't always like what I see when I see me. I see my outfit at times and my rolls, or my inappropriate big shirts. I feel like I have to change, I have to change who I am (not to fit in because freedom yoga is very accepting) but to feel comfortable in this setting, to feel comfortable being seen and maybe even being judged (even without intentions of it.)

I am not the best at poses, far from it actually. I lose balance at times, sometimes I stop or pause or even quit. sometimes I get distracted with my space and background.

Sometimes while on the mat I notice things from the low level that I want to change. I want to clean; I get distracted by it all.

But I know if my camera is not on.... I challenge myself less. I give up on myself easier because I don't feel held accountable. The teachers can't help me if they can't see me. Connections are harder to make when I am just a picture and name on the screen, instead of me live.

I am working on seeing me and being.

Being on camera, I don't always love what I see and I get distracted but I am working on taking the courage to just be me and show up and let that be enough.

Lena Ayala-Velasquez
March 4 · 21

Shared with Your friends

👥

This past month was live classes. I was able to join for ones that went with my wonky schedule, everyday certain ones served me. I was able to experience many teachers and people and my kids even joined in on the yoga. Yes, all 4 kids joined yoga days.

My husband even joined a bit.

Being live with people is a different feeling and accountability and realness, yes even through zoom.

BONUS! freedom yoga had their own challenge last month. Who will make it on to their mat the most, I came in second place with 36 times! I wasn't trying to win 1st or second place. I was just trying to make the most of my free opportunity. I was just trying to reach my goal of making yoga a daily habit for myself.

I have become stronger, I have so much to learn and grow.

My daughter and I were working out one day and she said "woah you can reach your feet like that" and I realized wow, I can.... I couldn't before.

I have grown, it has been hard.

It's hard to show up. I was even very sore. Yoga is a work out. You are working your body in new ways. It has felt like exercise, it has felt fun, spiritual, peaceful and challenging.

I have experience energy healing, journaling, everyday dharma, connecting.

and, I am not ready to let this go.

Tonight/today was my last day of my free gift package.

I did think, how will I make the money to keep this in my life?

But I also knew, I will make it happen.

I cannot, not have this in my life.

I want to support the person who created this, I want to support these teachers and this community. I want to grow with the people here. I want this as a part of my story, because-it is now.

I am so very thankful and grateful. To freedom Yoga, to Kim. To surrendered healing/Adelina, to the gratitude challenge. To myself and my family.

Last month's theme was about walking your path and this month the theme is spirituality.

Everything I am engaging in is in alignment with me, where I am at and where I want to go.

Every yoga class has connected to a part of me: meditation, prayer, journaling, resting, exercise, fun, family, community, challenge, peace, theme, focus, flexible schedule, options

I will admit I haven't always been on camera. Sometimes I get more distracted by seeing me on the screen. Sometimes I feel comfortable. But I am so proud. I am so happy. I am so thankful. And I am so ready, for more. I am ready to step more into who I am, who I am meant to be and continue to grow.

Lena Ayala-Velasquez
July 10 · 21
Shared with Your friends

Today after class, the checkout question was "what from class/your mat today was most enjoyable?"

It may sound strange but for me today what was most enjoyable was how sore I am. Because the sore body is showing and telling me just how much I have been slacking off in the past and just how hard I have been working, this month especially.

This month there is a "who can make it to the mat most challenge" and honestly it was just the motivation I needed, because paying monthly for my membership-I have been skating by.

I say this because with this challenge I am now doing more than I was doing before. Before this challenge I was trying to make it to my mat daily, at least once, for the 30minute sessions. Mostly mornings because I love starting my day with yoga in the morning.

With this challenge, I am doing multiple yoga classes almost every day.

I am joining on camera more; I am pushing myself and leaning into being seen. I am connecting more. I love check in and check out questions.

I am so excited for all of the free new classes next week; I feel like the "title" of each one speaks to me/my personality/my alignment and my soul.

I absolutely love being a member of the freedomyoga community.

as someone who suffers from chronic pains, this really helps me. It supports me. I am here because

I feel like spiritually, mentally, physically I want to be more peaceful and stronger- this helps me with that. I am nowhere near perfect. I know not "one" thing is a cure or "fix all" for anything.... but I have really found people I care about here. I have found practices that help improve me and my daily life.

I am so thankful

10.20.21
Self-care this week has looked like many different things
Some is daily practice and some is moment to moment for me
I have been very intentional about my energy and time
What matters to me is at the front of my mind
Daily journaling and gratitude are necessary
Morning yoga, time outside, going to the park- moving my body
Thoughtful food choices, cleaning and clearing
Getting more aligned with me and my truth- more being seen and less hiding
Celebrating all of the little things
Celebrating life and people, is important to me

Wearing my own clothes, make-up or not
Embracing my natural hair- not straightening it as much
Jumping rope, with my daughter
Saying yes and saying no- looking within for the answer

10.25.21
I feel balanced and harmonious when I accomplish things on my to do list
When I accomplish things on my vision board,
when I get through any part of the check list
I feel harmonious and balanced when I flow
When I get enough sleep, I can feel it in my soul

When I think of all I still want and still haven't done
Those are the obstacles that I face in accepting where I am and not feeling good enough
Thinking of the future, sometimes holds me back
Fortune telling can be depressing- I need to stop doing that

My kids, my husband and my family
Are all more deserving of my time and energy
Working out deserves my time

But It's hard to make it past just being a thought in
my mind
Finishing this book, deserves my energy right now
Because finishing this book matters to me and it
does not feel good that it hasn't yet worked out

Too many distractions are in my way
The phone out of habit, the mindless scrolling
throughout the day
The past, the future, the what I's
The shame, the guilt, the inner critic

In the shower is where I can be most distraction
free
In the shower, with my music, fully allowed to be
me

I have so many priorities
My work commitments, money invested in
places/people and things
My family is my top priority
Paying bills matters so much, unfortunately
Writing daily and reflecting -is something I can't
miss
Gratitude for me is something I live with

11.1.21
My distractions come in many forms
House cleaning and all of life's chores
Sick kids and illness
Doggie duties and the "to do" list
Feeling tired is a distraction
Social media – is a big distraction
Procrastination and longing
It all gets to me

11.15.21
The pandemic is something I like to overlook,
avoid and ignore
I would rather not deal with the constant change
of rules so we stay in and away from others
When we go out, we mostly keep to ourselves
We live with our truth on the tips of our tongues-
so we can know how to be with anyone else

So much is changing in my life
 So many moving pieces, all the time
Am I excited or struggling?
Through it all, I am embracing

11.29.21
Today my inner critic has a lot to say

I like to think I am a positive person but this
question has me feeling many ways
I am lazy and need to do more
I am too fat; I can't afford that- I should be playing
smarter
I can't self-publish again
My dreams are too hard to accomplish
I'll never have enough money to go back to school
I have too much junk that I'll never use
I am a hoarder
I am a libra and never for sure
I am ruined and can't be healed
I will always be broken and unable
I am not enough
I am too old to complete some stuff
I have to hide my truth
Because people won't accept me if they really
knew

I am judging myself more harshly at certain times
Like when people want to hang out but I have to
explain why we can't, as if they don't know why
I feel I have to be upfront about my beliefs and
truths
I feel like I know I'll be judged, so I avoid by giving
an excuse

I am harsh on myself for feeling this way
Like its not ok to be ok

When I know where others stand and if I know we differ
I just don't see why bother

My moral codes consist of honesty, gratitude and be intentional
My moral codes consist of practicing what I preach, show up as I am and be a life-long learner
I am all about living moment to moment
I have always lived by "treat others how you want to be treated"
But lately that thought process is changing
I am accepting people as they are and leaving our connections where they leave me
Honesty is policy
Everything is meant to be

If the pandemic were a person – it would be someone who regularly frustrates/disappoints and angers me
Its not the people-we are all human dealing with this reality
But the rules, the fears, the distrust, the grief

The disrupt, the pain, the way it divides and hurts
so many
That gets to me
That upsets me

I can proudly and shockingly say-
No one really upsets me these days
Despite the differences, I am at ease
But if the pandemic were a person- I would name
them quickly

12.6.21
My oldest daughter asked if we were going to
have stocking stuffers and gifts this Christmas, or
if we were too poor
I realized then, how I have been using my words
I realized then, how my words matter
I realized then I needed to change my language
At first, I had said, we are too poor
What was I trying to prove? What point was I
trying to make?
For them not to expect too much because I don't
want them to get their hopes up

But then I said, its not that we are poor
We can afford things

But right now, we have prioritized other priorities
Right now, material things aren't what we want to
mean most
We are invested in the life we are creating and
that means we have to use our money in different
ways
It doesn't mean we lack
We have a home, food, gifts, a tree, -all of that

I had to hear my kids say it
To really hear it and reframe it
I am so sorry for the example I have been, in that
way
I am so thankful for growth and change

I have been making my back pain say so much
about me
That I am not better than my old stories
That I have not truly healed
That I have not made progress for real
I have allowed my pain to hold me back
To curl up and sit in fear, scared to feel it
Scared to trigger more
So, I have been in depression and unsure
I have been questioning all of my growth
I have been spiraling out of "control"

I am reminding myself, I always have a choice
I am reminding myself, I can always use my voice
I am doing the best I can
Sometimes, I am just human
Sometimes I am not my best self
Sometimes I need help

I want to say no to the habitual habits of holding
my phone
I want to say no to the mindless scrolling
I want to say no to giving up
I want to say no, to yelling or raising my voice
I want to say yes to sleep
I want to say yes to school and money
I want to say yes to myself
I want to say yes, to help

8.9.21
Grab a few items from the room you are in, what
would you put on an altar. Things to manifest at
this time?

I chose cdb deep sleep capsules, virgin Mary,
stuffed dog, my book healing while hurting, tiny
book deck of cards, new bike tube and a plant.

These all symbolize different things for me.

I want more sleep so that I can be a better me and have better health.

The dog represents a new family member and a dream come true for our family.

I want to write more books and embrace what already is.

New bike tube means I want to fix what is broken, get exercise, do things a s a family, fix what I can and ask for help when I know I need support. I want to learn to do new things.

The deck of cards is because one day I want to create a deck of cards or a motivational calendar or planner one day. I want to honor all of my callings.

Virgin Mary because I want to lean into faith more. I want more clarity. I want to trust in the unknown more.

Plants, because I want to get outside and into nature more. I am changing my story of gardening. I can keep plants alive. Our garden will grow and feed us.

Coach- I want to live it.

Dream home, I want to be intentional about my vision so I can see it and dream it and make it real. I want to learn about cbd.

I want to learn to drive.

8.9.21
I am a healer
A learner, a teacher, an author, a mother, a wife, a sister, a daughter, a coach

I am authentic, honest, observant, connected and a writer

I am gratitude

I make it happen
For me and for others

I am mindful
I am poetry
I am truth

I am learning, I am sharing

What I noticed is-
A lot around my room – is what I want to see
Things that motivate and inspire me
A lot around the house- is what I use to pray for

Yoga mat, plants, own spaces, wealth, dreams,
family, health and comfort

Vision board, safety and happiness

I could die tomorrow.
I have dreams to make real. I have lives to touch. I
have family to enjoy.

Taking forward steps
And enjoying here and now.

If you had unlimited time and money, how would your days look like? What would you be doing? Who would you be with? What would you love?

_____

_____

_____

_____

_____

_____

_____

_____

_____

OVERWHELM

February 22 · 21

I met Jennifer last year, virtually when Barb Klein invited me to the group/challenge. I feel honored to have been a part of the first overcoming overwhelm challenge and I continue to join any time Jennifer leads groups. I have made new connections and friends thanks to this group and space and community. I have strengthened relationships through the challenges. I join, not to win prizes but I did win a prize before and it was so amazing. I am so thankful for how Jennifer shows up so authentically and full of gifts. I am so thankful to have this new challenge this February to help bring in this new year of 2021

September 30, 2020 ·

I did this challenge back in June. I decided I wanted to do it again because I missed the interactions and community in this group. When I first did the challenge before I wasn't feeling overwhelmed but I wanted the help for when I would need it again. Since last time, I have had my anxiety and stress and overwhelm creep back in at times. I always love a challenge and I love learning and growing . I love Jennifers support, guidance, knowledge. Coaching, energy.

I am not working right now, I thought I would be but then COVID. I started this year being a virtual assistant but then COVID. Up until last year I was and still always consider myself a teacher.

Up until this year my story has always been I have severe anxiety and it crippled me so much. My thoughts, my actions, my everything. The past few years I have really been working on me. On my healing and changing my stories. This year I am really working on ME. Not me the mom or the teacher or the wife or the coparent or the daughter or the girl with severe anxiety depression.

This year I am just working on me. Who I am outside of the titles and roles.

Lena Ayala-Velasquez Overcoming Overwhelm Challenge

October 2, 2020 ·

my daughter just asked "mom, when do you have meditation with the woman from the other day? I don't want to miss that"

Lena Ayala-Velasquez

September 28, 2020 ·

Shared with Your friends

I am committed to doing everything in this challenge to become the person I want to be.

I know I have said this before, the last time. And I did.

So, it appears to be true that I am always trying to become who I want to become.

it's a process, but the progress is there,

so happy to be here and thankful I made it to the live zoom call.

assignment two: I have been practicing all month long (and longer) today is no different. Plan to fail and keep trying anyways

assignment 3: be an encourager to yourself...I have done this several times today. this is one of the hardest and easier things today I encouraged myself to workout, in the morning! that was just 1:) but it got done

ASSIGNMENT FOUR:

*How does the person you want to become...

-I want to become the person who has her stuff together. Who is confident and courageous. I want to become so peaceful that it can't be disrupted. I want to become my best self.

*How does the you, you want to be -Move through the world?

• she moves with grace, confidence and power. She moves quickly and yet calm enough to soak it all in.

*Interact with their loved ones and friends?

• she is a listening ear, she helps make connections, she lifts others up and she knows when to create space and love from a distance when it isn't serving her.

*Deal with adversity and challenges?

-with an open mind, with love, with understanding and light and knows there is room to grow

*Deal with money?

she is investing in experiences and not things. she is saving to buy a home. she is working from home and creating income. she is not scared of making too much or not enough

*Order their day?

she moves with flexibility but there's a rhythm she enjoys

*Look like, speak like, & affect the world around them?

• she looks glowing, peaceful, calm, smiley. she affects the world around by good vibes and raising vibrations. she brings peace and happiness to those around her.

*What do they never skip?

-she does not skip time to herself to write, she doesn't skip the moments without the phone and social media, she doesn't skip outside time

*Make other people feel in their presence?

she makes them feel calm, safe, happy and curious

ASSIGNMENT FIVE: Spend two minutes before bed or as you fall asleep feeling what it feels like to be that person! (Do not try to figure out HOW are you going to become them. Just feel what it feels like to BE them. The how will come later!)

*I am going to try to take a nap and completed this but will again before bed and in the morning

Try to do this tomorrow evening as well. (Bonus points for mornings!) (That's a total of 2 to 4 minutes of homework each day! SEE? I told you this would be easy!)

(If you would like to, I would love to hear some of the words that describe future you in the comments below!)

future self, who I am becoming/working on:

- ♦ RESTED
- ♦ balanced
- ♦ peaceful
- ♦ zen
- ♦ determined
- ♦ author
- ♦ healthy
- ♦ energized
- ♦ productive
- ♦ nourished
- ♦ focused
- ♦ clear
- ♦ coach"

6.29.20

I would say the title of my life was "overwhelm. "

I don't necessarily feel this now. My journey of overwhelm has been many years, many stories. This past year I have been in counseling and I have been in coaching. I have overwhelmed in all areas of life. Especially with health, doctors, leaving jobs, and now this pandemic

The person I want to be, in the world is relaxed, calm and happy.
She has written books.
She is loving, present, and engaged.
She is spreading joy and positivity.
She makes others feel heard, welcome, safe, comfortable, and positive.
She is coachable, flexible and takes action.
She has a rhythm but not routine.
She never skips "I love you, walking to the door"
She is clean, dressed casually and feels good.
She is someone people want to be around.
She is known for smiling.
She is inspirational,
She motivates, supports, and helps others.

The traits of the person I am working to become is rested, active, present, healthy and zen.

I am here in this challenge because although I
don't feel too overwhelmed in life right now. I
know it will always come up. I want to learn new
things for my toolkit, I want to make connections
and seize the opportunity.

7.1.20
I am doing well
I am a little overwhelmed.
But every day I am working towards the me I want
to be
And the life I want to live.
I am happy to be here.

I am overwhelmed with all that isn't working.
I missed a call this morning, I made it here late.
I knew to put alarms, but I didn't- thinking id
remember. And I didn't.

I am needing a break from screens.
I am needing more sleep.
I am wanting to see the environment I desire
(Light, clean, beauty, no clutter)

"Make 2020, the year-you finally do it"
Whatever it, is

Do it

7.9.20
From my experience, my story is....
Many
I am a coach, a mom, a step-mom, I work to create
blended families and new meaning, I am bonus
mom, there is stigma

Through all my passions
I want to serve people as a whole
As they are
How we can grow and feel better
To live our best life
Greatness through the good and bad-together
There is no bad
I want to help others- support educate and love

I have too many callings

How did I end up here: physical therapy, chiro,
don't take over the counter medicine?
Holistic, not done with doctors
But done with doctors
I want more herbalism, holistic health and
nutrition

8.13.20
"I am not a morning person" is a limiting thought
Especially when I want to be a morning person, it
is what I want

I want to be committed
I want to want it
(To lose 15 pounds)
I guess this is a limiting belief and story I've been
telling myself

9.28.20
I am joining again because its always valuable

One word I want to feel is: rest(ed)
I want to embody the word rest
"I am rest"

10.7.20
You have to be wealthy to have a coach, is what
used to be my thought
It used to be what I knew to be true

10.12.20
Write all the negative beliefs you have:

I don't have enough money
I keep getting hit with financial hardship
I can't afford it
I get walked all over
Expect the worst
The other shoe will drop

2.22.21
Love yourself challenge, 5-day free challenge

Whatever you are saying and seeing in yourself is
what shows up.
Write out your negatives:

I am always sick
I have severe anxiety
I have uncurable back pain
I am poor
I am broken
I can't sleep
I am unhealthy

Money makes me feel safe and relieved

The me I want to be is an author, a coach, a present mother, a teacher, peaceful and zen, flexible, honest, true, happy and playful

I feel inspired and that makes me feel like I want to move my body

I haven't panicked about money, relationships, coparenting, beauty, school, work, anxiety or pain in awhile

Lena Ayala-Velasquez
January 20 · 21
Shared with Your friends

:busts_in_silhouette:

Last year I was a part of the "overcoming overwhelm" challenge with Jennifer white.

In the last challenge I won a prize about reclaiming space with Paul socket.

His content, coaching, knowledge and support is exactly what I need and want to stay in alignment with where I want to be and with where I have been going and working towards.

I feel so thankful to have taken the risk to try something new and I feel so thankful to have made the time. Let's be clear, I made the time because I made a commitment to someone else, I felt honored to win a prize----a prize that spoke to my soul, made it more exciting.

Even with all the greatness...It took being courageous to step out of my comfort zone. I am so thankful I set my alarm, or time would have passed me by and I would not have made it on.

I am so thankful I was able to text the other person who won the challenge and that we both got to show up and just be us-as people.

Not as mom or stepmom or blending families or wives or whatever titles...just as our names, as who we are.

It felt so nice. It was a great time. It was fun, funny, comfortable, I learned so much. It is true that a new relationship was born.

Thank you barb, Jennifer, Paul and Ileana. Today was possible because of you all. The connections and opportunities and invitations. I am so excited for what's to come. I am so grateful for all that is from today.

I am thankful to have today's experience as a part of my wellness Wednesday, my wealth is health, my winning Wednesday.

so much wonder, why's and wisdom.

I am thankful to have today's experience as a part of my 2021 beginning.

thankful, grateful, blessed

Lena Ayala-Velasquez

March 5 · 21

Shared with Your friends

Free Friday

Free isn't always Free.

Sometimes giving a book means trading, means it will still end up in the right hands, means I can give back, Means I have something to give, Means I still get the message out, means income is still possible-just in ways I didn't think of or know to be options.

who doesn't love FREE? I love free, I try to take advantage of free.

I was asked if I wanted to give a book as a prize for a challenge. The overcoming overwhelm challenge.

I had so many thoughts "What an honor"

"This is a way I can say thank you, because I have participated in the free challenges several times"

"Other authors offered books. An author who means a lot to people, who is seasoned. I can't compare. Will anyone be excited for my book, when I am just me."

Financial Freedom, is a goal many have.

make connections, open up, trust your truths and your journey, follow your heart and put yourself out there

it's scary. All the negative thoughts will hold us back if we allow it.

so, be brave.

Today I said yes.

what an honor that someone asked me to give a prize in a challenge! someone asked me to share my gift. How awesome that I was thought of, that I was asked.

I wonder what it took that person, to even ask me.

so many thoughts and feelings.

I feel so thankful. for the opportunity, for working through the hard thoughts and for courage to say yes ☺

Lena Ayala-Velasquez
December 18, 2020 ·
Shared with Your friends

Hello Friday

My husband was up and out the door at 6am. Back to work.

Let me tell you, I am thankful for the Friday last week that wasn't this and I am thankful for the days that weren't today.

I don't miss hearing him leave at early hours and then not being able to sleep.

I don't miss my mind racing- waiting to hear he made it ok and is safe.

I don't miss the thoughts (there's homelessness and break ins that happen over there, more often than we hear about.)

I know he's doing a job that is taxing on his hands and body. As he cleans ovens. It really is a two-person job but I am thankful for him.

I am thankful for how hard he works- he does side jobs/extra jobs to make a little more income.

I am thankful he has a job and has extra opportunities.

I will always feel he deserves more because I know how hard he works and how hard the work is.

I don't miss Athena up at 6 realizing her dad is gone and screaming/crying because she wants him (it took a while to calm her this morning.)

I made my rounds after I couldn't go back to sleep and covered all the kids with extra blankets because the house was freezing and they were not warm enough.

I avoided my phone-trying to rest my mind.

But all I kept thinking was: back to reality.
He's back to work. He's back to working hard.
Wondering what work hours and shifts and things will look like these days.
Wishing he didn't start until Monday, at least.
Knowing the income is needed.
Praying his health is recovered enough and wishing I could know it won't be compromised again.

Yesterday was what felt like our most normal day since a positive test result last Monday and working through c19 symptoms.

I am thankful he had the past 11 days off- even if it wasn't a vacation or anything. The fact that he had days of rest, self-care and recovery -were much needed. He's been working hard ever since high school. He's been working this job plus side jobs since high school. These past 11 days were his only real rest.

Because any days off are usually still work days of some sort.

This time he took days for real rest. Some.

I hope this experience makes him value himself more and I hope people at work value each other more.

Mental health, physical labor, - it's all so taxing. I'm thankful he's feeling recharged and well. I am thankful he's feeling great to be back at it. I am thankful he's so positive and happy.

My prayers to all those returning, to all those still recovering and to everyone else. Werner your job is labeled essential or not. We are all essential. Every life.

Hello Friday.
Faith over fear
Flowing, not forcing

What is financial freedom?
What does freedom mean to you?
What are you needing to find courage to face?
How can you make Friday feel like fri-yay?
How can you live a fuller life?
Find yourself, love yourself, take care of you.

Gratitude for me is being thankful for all of the
good, bad and in-between

Gratitude saved me, before I could even articulate
it. When I was younger, even older.
Lena Ayala-Velasquez
March 4 · 21
Shared with Your friends

what are you proud of yourself for? This past
week?
-I am so proud my husband and I made time for us
-I am proud I started working on my mom's book
more

-I am proud for showing up and taking advantage of the free challenges this week
-I am proud of celebrating 17 years of our love story and 11 years married
-I am proud of showing up to yoga almost every day this past month and several times twice a day
-I am proud of grace/guilt and flowing not forcing
What are you thankful for today? right now?
-I am thankful for open-source wellness group
-I am thankful for courageous life society
-I am thankful for overcoming overwhelm group
-I am thankful for surrendered healing community
- I am thankful for mothers quest community
-I am thankful for all of the coaches, social media, free opportunities, affordable opportunities, connections, open doors, growth, new relationships
-I am thankful for the SHIFT group
-I am thankful for free food, family support, family laughs, my hard-working husband, time for me, time for us, time for family, changes, challenges and all the blessings big and small
_I am thankful for life, for this new day, for alarms set, for goals and plans and dreams and getting things done
****

you can ask yourself these questions anytime 😊

In this moment, what are you grateful for?

_____

_____

_____

_____

_____

_____

_____

_____

_____

COURAGEOUS

Julie was sharing about this free challenge by Jessica stong. I was interested right away because I had heard Julie talk about Jessica Stong before. It was a Free 5-day morning makeover challenge She is a different time zone than me, but for me that wasn't an issue once I got the hang of it. (why do I share a detail such as a time zone difference? Because, that could have easily been a factor to not show up, to not join. I could have let that stop me, and I would have missed out on so much.)

One thing I had hoped to learn in this challenge was to train my brain to become consistent with practices my heart knows I need, and my soul knows it wants. This challenge was one of those things I know I needed and wanted.

At the end of the challenge, I was so proud that I made it each day to watch the teachings and take notes. I have not embodied it all or done everything exact, but I got what serves me.

After this challenge was over, we were offered the opportunity to become founding members as a bonus if we joined the group coaching program. I thought to myself "there's so much more I can gain from this. I would love to be a founding member-what an honor. The price is only going to go up, so if I think I can't afford it now-I really wont later. I don't want to regret passing this moment up." So, I became a member.

I now have access to the tools, I get to be coached by someone amazing, I get to meet and connect with others, I get to lock in this rate, I get to be a founding member. I get to become a better me.

Right now, my current morning routine looks like: check my phone to see if I have messages and reply if I do, scroll through social media, check my text to do list, check my daily planner, check my calendar, make my bed and clean my room, open windows and curtains though out the house, unplug night lights, walk my husband outside when he leaves to work, feed kids, put on tv...

Jessica Stong has said so many things that really stuck out to me.

"You don't have to live in chaos anymore. Emotions are our guidance system. Choose thoughts that serve you"

"We are not limited by our circumstances"
"We get the choice to choose everyday"

In this challenge everything she is saying is aligning with me. "You have to deliberately think new thoughts. Your brain must believe the thoughts you offer it. The thought has to feel better. If you don't believe it, it will create negative thoughts and emotions"

One question that has been on my heart and mind is, what is my pandemic/covid instruction manual? I decided I would and was already taking on this pandemic reality, in that way-without even realizing.
We are all in this together. As in, no one has a manual or instructions on exactly how to be during this time. We each will live life and this time through our own lenses and manuals. I am figuring out what my manual is.

FOUNDING MEMBER

How can I not lock that in?
I get to be part of something that I feel is so
important.
How am I here, right now at this time?
To be considered a founding member, how is this
my life?
I can't let this pass me by
I have learned to love Jessica stong and how she
serves in my life.

It was today when we were asked if we wanted to
create a new story
If we wanted to join in on life membership, in the
courageous life society.
It was today when I decided, I didn't want to miss
out
When I decided I knew I needed this help...
6.22.20 7.21.20

SHE SAY'S

She says I can love my life despite anything that
might come up for me
She says we can learn to love it all-even the
challenging and overwhelming things

I want a life that I can love
I don't want to hate my circumstances
she says you have to decide to love your life
In order to change my circumstances

I hear you Jessica, so thankful to hear you live

I will not hustle anymore
I believe this can get me new results
I will show up as I am
I will create new thoughts, to feel new things and
take action
6/26/20

CIRCUMSTANCE

Because of my back pain I can't exercise and
become healthier
I can't lead by example and my kids ending up like
me is my fear.

This is my circumstance
It's hard to believe anything else when I can't.

I know I was made for more
More than this pain, this story for sure.

I was made to grow through this
I was made to heal from this.
I can't write down all I am hearing and learning
from Jessica stong
But what I will say, is I can listen to her all day
long.
I want to listen, just to raise my energy
My energy in my home and in me.
So many pages of notes
So thankful for the replay-because there's so
much, I want to know.
6/29/20

EMOTIONAL VIBRATIONS

Emotions are just vibrations
And vibrations are powerful
Everything is energy
Our thoughts are everything

I am trying to create the life of my dreams
I have to try new things in order to reach new
everything
6/29/20

242

MORNING THOUGHTS

I am practicing my morning thoughts
Right now, I am just noticing them for what they
are.

I want to sleep longer
I'd like to shower.
How do I make it worth it?
Wanting it is good enough, so-I do it.
I want to dye my hair but I don't need to
I have to think of everyone's hair, I can't think of
mine too.
Its Monday, what is my anchor thought and goals
My back hurts, is what I really know.

Then I scroll through my phone...

I meditate on my anchor thoughts for this year
"Flowing not forcing", "faith over fear"
Make it happen
Create my zen.

I want to have a morning and night-time routine
I want to eat better, that's the goals for this week.

I am grateful for waking up,

For my husband cuddling with me.
For my family,
For this group.
For a new day.

Right now, my routine, I can do on autopilot
I wake up-take everything off of the bed, to fix it.
I open the curtains and windows and front doors
for fresh air and light
I unplug all nightlights.
I go to the bathroom to do my morning things
I get dressed and wake the kids-make sure they
eat.
I scroll through social media and check my planner
for the day
I check my calendar then clean, so I can say I was
productive today.

I want to create a nighttime routine
I want to go to bed by 10:30.
Maybe read a book with the kids at 8:30
So, the last thing we all see isn't screens.
I want to put the phones down by 8:30
Leo will start sleeping in his own bed, finally.

Why do I want to change my nighttime routine?

I feel like it will help me be a better me.
I want to get up earlier
I want to enjoy my days longer.
I want to feel better in the morning
I want to feel like I am not rushing.
7/6/20

ACCOMPLISHMENT THIS WEEK

An accomplishment to celebrate this week
Is building new furniture, throwing things out and
unpacking.
Creating the space, I want to see
Little by little, it will get complete.

I am thankful my family took a trip to Taho for the
first time
We made it there and back safely, that plays a big
part of my mind.
I was able to check off "flowing not forcing"
Also creating the life and home I wish to see.
7/18/20

MAKE IT THROUGH, IS ALL I WANT TO DO

Is it bad, that this week- I just want to make it
through?

I can't come up with an anchor thought, I don't
really even care to.
My yesterday and this morning have been
challenging
So many emotions, non-helpful thoughts and
worries.

We can't control the circumstance
But we can control how we think about it.

Trying to do everything is exhausting
I cannot say affirmations I don't believe.
I can't let my failures determine my future,
because they don't
If I don't think they will, then they won't.
7/13/20

CURRENT STORY THOUGHTS

My current thoughts and stories
They say so much about me

"If my husband would stop drinking, our life would
be better"
"I should get my BA, by now I should have had my
masters"
"I will be a better role model if I go back to school"

"I want to lead by example "
"My husband deserves to be happier"
"He deserves a different job if he wants to change careers"
"If I didn't have back pain, I could participate in yoga"
"If I didn't have back pain, I could exercise and lose weight and be peaceful"
"If my mom stopped smoking, I would enjoy her being around more"
"If I get a new computer, I will be happier"
"If I get a new computer, it will get the tasks done that I need and want"
"If I get rid of the clutter, we will all be happier with it gone"
7/21/20

WHAT IF, I HAD THE COURAGE- TO DARE?

What if I had the courage to dare
To not go by my planner or calendar.
What if I don't tell the kids "Wait" or "hold on"
What if I do not go on social media, all day long.
What if we gave up screens for the day?
What if I threw things away?
What if we gave up on junk food?
 What if we organized the dining room?

What if we go through all the bins of things?
 What if I started a bog and not just Facebook posting?
What if, I get my poetry book together to publish my fist book?
What if, I practice driving and we got rid of the Subaru?
What if, we bought a new small car, off the lot?
What if I had no phone for the day- what about all of us?

Here what's I want...
No soda, no junk, no gas station runs.
I want to go on runs in the morning
I want to go with my husband and start exercising.

What if I had the courage to dare?
Do one thing each day that makes me scared.
One thing each day that helps me face a fear
I am so ready, I guess that is why I am here.
7/16/20

WHAT I KNOW TO BE TRUE

I feel like and what I know to be true

That during this time of the pandemic, so far- my
life is going in the direction I have always wanted
it to.
For the first time ever, I have felt safe enough to
leave the kids home alone
Sure, I didn't go too far and we have family all
around-but I am working on my fears and growth.
I am working on allowing them to be without me
I am working on my trust in society.
I have invested in me
I am in groups and receiving coaching.
I have allowed change to take place in the house
I have thrown so many things out.
I am practicing, even more
In what it means to be holistic, even more than
before.
We are more active, more on the bikes
We have made trips, we have traveled and gotten
in family time.
Everyone kind of has their kids at home for school
I am a stay-at-home mom and wife and
entrepreneur.
Income comes in many forms
I am all about self-care, self0growth and not about
how I perform.
I know it's only been 6 months but I am growing

I am flowing, I am loving the me I am being -the me I am showing.
I can manage my brain around the things that are happening
There's so much I can't control but I am in charge of me.
I am allowing myself to dream
I am allowing myself to embrace the beauty during hard things.
I keep hearing "what you focus on grows" and I know that to be true
I am tired of the negative, scarcity, pain-I am ready for something new.
7/27/20

WHAT MATTERS TO YOU?

What thoughts, ideas and projects matter to you? Why does it matter to you?

Organizing spaces, creating the home inside of the home-is really on my heart
Plant based diet, eating better- is also what I see in my cards.
Yoga commitment, meditation practice
Night/morning routine---night is when the next day begins.

I see myself creating a blog
Launching a course and writing a book.
I see myself in coaching training
Making money to live the life of my dreams.
I see myself getting holistically educated
So many spaces and places I want to be an
affiliate.

Things we want to do, don't always get done
This is not failure, it's a chance to change our
thoughts.
We can't complete all of our tasks and dreams at
once
We have to take it, one by one.
7/29/20

ONE THING

This month I am having a hard time picking one
thing to commit to
I feel like I know what I should pick but I am
resisting that truth.

Unpacking bins from moving, find space to create
space
Let go, declutter- the signs are all in my face.

I care about this because having a clean space
makes me feel better
I am too comfortable with the thought/joke of
being a hoarder.
I love knowing that I have things
I am blessed materialistically.
And that wasn't always the case for me
I love knowing we have so much as a family.
But I also know, being organized, brings me peace
I want my environment to inspire and feel good- I
want to love what I see.
8/2/20

LETTING GO MEANS...

What if I get rid of stuff and want it later?
Letting go means I wasted money, holding on
makes me a hoarder.
Who can I give this stuff to?
So much is gently used and some still brand new.
So much no longer serves me
So much no longer serves the vision for my future
reality.
How can I keep it?
How can I create space to keep it?
Why am I keeping it?

I don't need it.
I have been living without so much that has been
boxed up and hidden
So why not let it go and finalize it.
What makes knowing its there bring me comfort?
Its not comforting to my eyes, it brings discomfort.
Feeling like less is more
Letting go means more space-open space and
closure.
No clutter, will feel good
I will be able to create the look I wish to see, the
one that feels good.
No more baggage
Its just stuff, stuff I have outgrown
One person's treasures, another's garbage
Keep what you need, give to those in need and let
the emotional ties go.

We moved here, back here in march of this year
After being gone for exactly a year.
I have lived here most of my life
I manifested it, again- this time.
The pandemic stopped us from being able to buy
new stuff
So many places are closed, so many businesses
won't open back up.

It's also been hard to get rid of stuff
Because all of the support groups and places to
give-aren't allowed to take stuff.
And people are scared to take used things
Scared of the illness that could be lingering.
There's no work, less work, less money
So much struggling.

The space here is different than before
Its not the same space anymore.
Less fits and nothing fit the same
And yet I am holding on as if that reality will
change.

Less is more, so they say
Circumstances will force us to let go of stuff and I
have to be ok.
8/3/20

OPTIONAL

Jessica stong says our thoughts are optional
She says how we want to feel is optional.
That we are in in control for how others respond
And that others can't make us feel anything, the
choice is ours alone.

Today, I am not focusing on my challenge
I am telling myself that other things are more
important.
How does that show up in other areas of my life,
she asks?
Am I avoiding? Maybe-I need to sleep
Not cleaning this mess is driving me crazy.
I have other commitments
I feel like I am failing at my to do list.
I feel like I am failing as a mom, wife and person
I feel like I am failing myself -not doing "anything"
today that's really important.
I know doing all I have done, helps me still
But these are all of my thoughts, this is what is
mentally real.
8/5/20

UNPACKING

Unpacking, I can do it later
but later, is always later.
I do not have space
But I have space to make the space.
That was too expensive to let go of
I can still use that, but will I? I haven't done so.
One day I will fit that again
But one day I may never fit that again.

That means something to me
But some no longer serves the life I am living and creating.
I'm too tired to get started
I'm tired of not making progress.
I need help
But I don't want anyone's help.
Bins save space
Bins take up space.
What's in the bins?
It's not like I am using it.
Clutter is ugly, frustrating, unhealthy and a waste
Once it done, I'll feel better, but its hard to get to that change.
I know I need to let go
But its hard for me to let go.
I want to love what I see
Right now, I don't like the picture that is reality.
Organization feels good
It will be easier to keep clean too.
8/7/20

PRODUCTIVITY

Productivity, feels like the word
It looks like things crossed off of the "to do" list, for sure.

Productivity feels good
It feels like I have done something that I am
supposed to.

My success of the week is going with the flow
Doing things outside of the one project I chose.
Things I have been wanting and needing to do
Like biking with the kids, less looking at the
planner but set alarms for things I have committed
to.

Right now, its easy to look over to the rooms and
feel overwhelmed and stressed
These are the emotions I feel about the project.
I have been avoiding this week, so far
I am just now looking at my goal for the week and
the week is almost over.
It's all do-able
To create a homework/workspace and de-clutter.

I did last weeks goal in one day
It only took a couple hours out of my Sunday.
I have looked at stores for desks but haven't loved
any
I have looked for a new computer but haven't
decided on any.

On the other side of all of this
I want to feel peace, success, spacious and
happiness.
But the hardest part about being productive
Is there's too much to do on my "to do" list.
8/12/20

COURAGE MEANS

To me courage means being scared and doing it
anyways.
I have to name it out loud, do it and then reflect
on the whole thing.
Many times, I am brave, is because my children
give me courage.
If I am encouraging them, I want to show it to
myself as well.
I want to lead by example and live in courage.
8/17/20

CELEBRATE TODAY

Today I want to celebrate speaking up
I want to celebrate being honest and not keeping
it, all bottled up.
I want to celebrate not holding on to the wonder

For not avoiding conversations that I know will
bring pain and anger.
For not avoiding talks that will bring up feelings I
would rather avoid
For making that choice.

Again, it has to do with my children
It has to do with advocating for them.
Its scary for us adults too
But in order to lead by example, facing fears is
something we have to do.
Its scary to ask for what we want and have to
negotiate
To ask for something when we know it will bring
an argument, bad feelings of sadness/anger and
pain.
Knowing the answer will be no and lead to a fight
But knowing you have to stand up for what you
feel is right.
To not want to cause friction
To not want to bring on pain or rejection.
But also, not wanting to be silent
Not wanting to wait or just settle- so you don't
stay silent.
8/19/20

MISSED OPPORTUNITY

The curiosity and idea again to want to start and Esty shop.
I should take advantage of Kristen Gennawey helping people do this.
Here we are in December of 2021 and I was never able to make it happen. I missed the opportunity. Life happens. Things change and that opportunity that once was has been no more. No, I didn't wait until now, I tried at the beginning of the year and months before that. It is one of the things I regret not investing in (because I had too much on my plate.) But that feeling of still wanting it and not having that same chance, eats at me way more than having too much on my plate before.

What is an opportunity you might have right now, that you are debating on but you know your heart really wants?
Can you say yes to your heart? Or will you live in regret?
8/20/20

NOT YET, DOES NOT MEAN THERE HAS NOT BEEN SUCCESS

In the courageous life society, we are asked, what are you celebrating today? What is preventing you from seeing the results you want?
Did you meet your <u>august</u> goals?

I am celebrating the kids starting school
I am celebrating having our oldest with us, every other week, it is a dream come true.

I have not met all of my goals, yet
The past two Saturdays, my weekly goals weren't met.
But I have done so much more this month towards it, that I haven't done in years of just wanting to
Right now, I see I have been avoiding some stuff I want to do.
I feel like I need the desk and bedframe before I can get organized
I have added other things to my plate when I said I wouldn't add more to my list, which already feels like there's not enough time.

I do many things to rest

Like going outside, putting the phone down and
getting the baby to nap.
When I want to rest, I turn off screens
I use essential oils to help with my wellbeing.
I get a massage or take a shower
I cancel plans and nap at different hours.
8/26/20

ONE DARE A DAY

I have made a list of things to choose from
To do 1 dare each day of this month.

Today is day one
I dare myself to finish day 1 workout and get
number 2 done.
I dare myself to start yoga
I did completed workout 1 and 2 but not yoga.
It's one thing a day, I have to follow the rules
I won't get the results I want, trying to do it my
way and not listening to what I am "supposed to."

I did not fail, I just need to choose one thing
My brain is saying I need to do more- that one
isn't productive enough
But it took me all day to complete what I did
complete

262

It was a real challenge, which lets me know I did enough.

****The confidence/dare challenge
pick one thing a day (6 days a week)
has to involve fear
write before and after
try to be consistent
these things can be whatever is a challenge to you. My list consists of so many things (don't tell the kids to wait, don't scroll social media all day, no junk food day, no screen day, start a blog, put on make-up, dress up, organize dining room, write my poetry book outline, practice driving, get rid of broken car, browse new cars, no phone for a day, no soda month, go on a morning run, go on a date night with my husband, go to the bird sanctuary, make a vision board, find the money to join soul care, go to burney falls, remove skin tags, go back to school, make a dentist appointment, potty train the baby, workout, yoga, sign up for doterra education, use my water jug, plant my Lilly plant, buy democracy jeans, take a bath, drink tea.....) your list is your list. Something small, you can do each day-that requires you to get over a fear or face the "I don't want to do this" feeling.

Our brains will tell us all sorts of things
"You haven't done enough"
"This is too little progress"
 "You won't succeed"
Celebrate each and every success
Stay in gratitude for all that is, and isn't.

Jessica says "what you focus on grows"
Look for the positive and reinforce all that you
know.

Something that works for me,
Is not removing temptation, and instead facing the
feelings they bring.
But sometimes I don't want the pressure
The choice, is always yours.
9/1/20

REHEARSED STORIES

My stories are so rehearsed and embedded into
me
These stories are what I know to be true of my
reality.

epidurals ruined me

my back pain wouldn't be what it is if I knew
better than to agree.
I am a product of drugs and poverty
I am poor and that's all I can ever be.
I am a mom to all
I have to save everyone.
A piece of me died when my dad died
Not having my BA and masters means I am
wasting time.
Cheating changed me
We can never be the good that we were because
of the painful memories.
I can't afford to eat healthy
I can't not worry.
My back pain won't allow me to work out or do
yoga
I need more classed, more certificates and degrees
to feel important.
I don't know it all, so I can't do it (why try)
I'm wasting the education I have by not working
all the time.
There's is no time for me, to even take a bath
That luxury can only be for the kids.
I want it but don't need it
I am not deserving to splurge on my own gifts.
I have to do it all or it won't be done right

We can't catch a break, especially during
pandemic times.
Life is unfair
No one really cares.
I have to hold it all together
If I don't, we won't stay together.
I have severe anxiety
I can't sleep.
I am the glue
I don't have a choice; I have to choose the things I
don't want to.
I am good at being the glue
I have to fix it for them, that's just what I do.
I get sick easily and it lasts forever
I have to compromise because I just don't deserve
better.
I'm not as important as his "real mom"
I can never be more than his "stepmom."
Covid won't let me work or live out loud
What now?

But there's so much more I want my new story to
be
I am just mom; I matter and I am as important as
she.
I can afford it

healthy eating is cheaper than illness.
I am never too old for school
I don't need to know it all and I can't be expected
to.
I am a lifelong learning, I am always learning
I am authentic, its ok to be me.
I am not my mom
I am learning from my mom.
My mom is an example
I am an example
I can be a morning person I believe that in this
work, there is transformation.

Do our stories make us who we are?
I believe our thoughts and our words matter
9/23/20

REFLECTION TIME

Its reflection times
To check back on this month of dares and see
what got done in this time.
I had a list of things I wanted to try
I also had a list not on the list but was on my heart
and mind.

I made connections with people from groups on
social media
I attempted to get the baby to eat new foods and
didn't overreact when she threw up.
I went bike riding
I even went with family.
I mailed gifts
I used door dash to send presents.
I joined soul care for one year
I did participate in daily dares.
I am in the tiny book course
I allowed help from family members.
I joined mama medicines 4-week opportunity
I joined to work with Lynda fitness with
beachbody.
Our desks never came and then the prices raised
and are out of stock
I got a new lap top.
Counseling changed to once a month
I have courageous conversations with another
mom.
I am a doterra oils specialist
I even got a certificate.
I took a bath and made time for me
I put on makeup, just for me.
I repotted my plants

Some with help and some by myself, I did it.
I went on a morning walk and jog
I took the kids on a couple of store runs.
I took some cbd deep sleep capsules
I portioned my food.
I tried yoga and pilates
I set some expectations and boundaries.
9/30/20

FEELINGS WHEN GROWING UP

Growing up, I feel like the house was always a
forever sh** show
We were allowed to express all feelings, no one to
tell us no
But we weren't taught how to deal with them
Just people who didn't want to deal with them
Not really cared for- just reacted to instead of
responded to
Anger got attention, sadness sometimes did too

Right now, this is what's connecting with me
I am sure there are other realities in my memories
9/30/20

PERMISSION TO BE

I want to give myself the permission to be silly
To play freeze tag with the kids and let my inner
child free.
A nap is not a sign of weakness
I deserve rest, even if others don't feel I need it.
Taking a break is not weak
And so, what if it is, what's wrong with feeling
weak?
10/7/20

RESPONSIBLE TO CARRY BURDEN

My birthday time is coming
It is always stressful for me.
I want to learn how to surrender
I don't mean be walked all over.
I mean to have acceptance
To have the courage.
I have all of these real feelings
Ones that don't bring on happiness or positivity.

I am not important as the other parent
This is to be expected.
It's always a fight
It's always about time.

270

But there's never enough time
I don't want more bad memories on my heart or
mind.
We will never win
I am a failure, but I can't quit.
Why did I put so much on my plate?
How can I get this story to change?

I want to move forward with healing
I need to free up energy.
My responsibility is to carry burden
That's what I have believed but I no longer want
that burden.
10/14/20

BIGGEST FEAR

My biggest fear is to make the wrong decision as a
parent
This fear keeps me stuck in in-action.
To me, worry shows I care
I am learning I have depended on others for
happiness and it's never felt fair.
I am practicing courage by doing differently
I am surrendering.
I am not fighting
I am trying not to overthink.

I wonder what life looks like without anxiety and
worry
I wonder if that could ever be my reality.
Worry takes so much from me
I am working on what I want my new normal to
be.
10/21/20

COACHES GIVE LIFE

Coaches give us tools, but we have to do the work
I know what you're thinking "so what do you pay
for?"
Truth is, you have to experience for yourself
I can only speak for me, no one else.
You get so much more than just tools
You get the like you never knew.
10/28/20

UNLEARNING CONDITIONS

Sometimes ignorance is bliss
Maybe I want to be this way during covid.
Because the news is all so scary
Like organ failure in kids called Kawasaki.
So, these days I am watching less news

I don't turn it on the way I used to.
I am not saying I don't want to be informed
I am saying, so much is unnecessary and the fear
(for me) has to be unlearned.
11/4/20

MY MANUALS

I am working on re-writing my manuals
Like not living from a place of hustle.
I am learning to believe
In everything I want to believe.
I am doing the best I can
Feeling guilty doesn't serve me, so I am letting go
of that.

I want letting go to be fun
I wonder then, what I could overcome.
11/25/20

THIS YEAR...

This year I am a re-covering people pleaser
This year, I am big on self-care.
This year, I will get the book out
So much has gotten done by now.
I will figure out what I want for 2021

Podcasting is free, I can do it-but I feel I need direction.
12/2/20

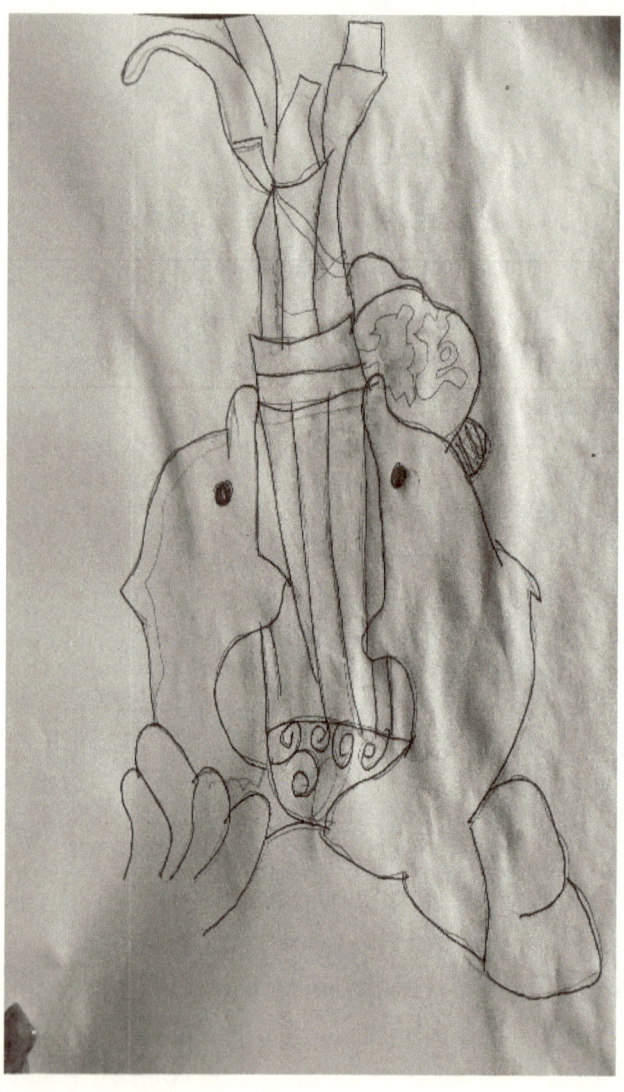

What fears do you have? Can you thank your fear and then move forward with courage?

_____

_____

_____

_____

_____

_____

_____

_____

_____

SURRENDER

Adelina Tancioco holds many titles. I met her though my work at Alternatives in Action. I was drawn to her workshop she was leading, we connected. Over time we connected through her Surrendered Healing Facebook page. I would join her free events and challenges. She is a spiritual life coach and inspirational speaker. One of the free events she led was called Transform through covid virtual pop-up healing center with 21 healers of color in June of 2020. I participated in several opportunities with her over the years. This year in 2021 the Facebook group was shut down; I was a bit sad. Ok, very sad. But we still connected through IG. I even became the social media connector for surrendered healing and it still feels unreal. It wasn't a position I was looking for, or even saw for myself. But people were coming to me, to do things like this over the last few years. I just never realized I had a gift in this way and that it mattered.

The reflections I am going to share are not in any specific order and they are nowhere near all of my story or journey with Adelina or surrendered healing. They are just some journal pages from over time.

SUFFERING IS OPTIONAL

Cancer.
Why my dad? Why my uncle? Why my mother-in-aw?

What could be the good news?
To write that book.
To help others, who may be going through what I am going through.
To know how to help my husband
To live life different.

I've thought about this a lot.
I am never whole about it.
I will never have complete understanding.
I still say but why? Why me?
Is suffering optional? can it be?

I am feeling rooted, faithful, home and present

I was made for this moment, this pandemic.
It was made for me
For me to have more clarity.

When I am in surrendered Sundays, I feel like I am
in church. I feel my messages come to me with
ease.
Right now, this will be offered the first Sunday of
every month and I am looking forward to it.
3/7/21

ADELINA WAS LIVE WITH MESSAGES

I have tears flowing, feels like I went to church. I
needed this.
It lets me know, everything is right on time and all
I have been doing is right on time.

One truth I walked away with today is that
nothing is coincidence.
And one action step I am taking in the next 24
hours will be to rest.
I am reminded, time and time again- that the
message repeats until we listen
9/30/20

ADELINA WAS LIVE

I love when she speaks. I miss church.
 I feel like I am in church when she speaks.
Everything is landing so much for me.
I have goosebumps
11/3/20

CALLINGS

We each have our own callings.
Right now, what's calling me is to teach, to write,
to help, to serve, to smile, to greet, to watch, to be
mom
1/10/21

Now to move on to surrender, in general...

Abundance to me is everything around me. It is
the ability to have the bills and debt I have. It is
the ability to pay them off. It is the life I live, the
people and places I get to be with.
I can bring awareness into my life by being
conscious and intentional. By being at peace,
knowing all is as it should be and listening to my
inner voice.

DIFFERENCES

People I love believe different than me
When it comes to this pandemic, we are all just
trying to be.
We are living different truths, trusts, paths,
experiences
I still love them.
But, can/will they still love me?
Where do breaking points come in, for others- and
for me?

Why does it matter?
5/25/21

HEART-WORK

I love being an author
For me, its my calling-my healing and it matters.
I love collaborating as a family
I love the feedback I have been receiving.
I love, my work- from the heart
I want to do so much more; this was just a start.
Life is too short
5/25/21

IT ALL MATTERS

I want to teach
But not with masks or shots for those who don't believe.
I miss going to church and connecting
I don't miss feeling like bad would come if we weren't attending.
I don't miss feeling obligated
I miss the songs, the feeling of the space and certain faces.

I want to work and get paid
Not just make enough to survive but thrive and enjoy every day.
I want to be here, home with the kids
I want my husband to always feel supported.

For 22 days I did daily meditation. Meditation is not easy. To find the time, to create the habit. But every time I tuned in, it felt like all the things I needed to hear, I could feel it all in my body- everything was making sense. I knew I needed to show up, for myself- in this way. And so, I did. And I am so happy I did. I learned so much. So much conformation, so much new perspective and learning.

5/25/21

MOMMY AND FAMILY

I am very interested in building my relationship
with my mother. When my dad was alive, this was
important to me but even more as he passed.
It was through this time of finding me outside of
my titles, that I was able to see my mom in a
different way. To see her as just human and not
within the titles I have held for her, or she has of
herself.

Lena Ayala-Velasquez
September 17 · 21
Shared with Your friends

I don't want the "busy" anymore
the too busy to be with my family
the "too much working" not enough living
the constant busy of people and crowds and no
space to move
I want the empty

the village/community of people who trade and
take care of each other

a place where you know where your food comes
from and that it is healthy and available
I want busy building community, people doing
what they love. Happy energy. real emotions but
togetherness to hold space to pull through those
times with grace and forward movement.

I want to be able to do what I love. Live what I
love.
to have time for all that matters.
to make enough money for what's important to
me and right now that means: seeing the
chiropractor at least 3 times a month, getting a
massage at least once a month, being able to buy
products when I want and need. I want to be able
to afford seeing the doctor I want. I want to own
my own home and have my loved ones close. I
want school from home. I want to be able to work
from home.
I want to go to school for herbalism, among so
many other passions.
I want to have less screens and more creeks. Less
time away and more time to be still.
I want more music and less sirens.
I don't want to stress about how to survive, how
to get by, how to make it through, not enjoying

work. I don't want to work just for money. I want to help make the world a better place.

I want to travel and see the world; with those I love. I want to know more than just where I have been and am. I want to know my family's history. I want to know the roots of me.
I want to know life of freedom, of support and health and wealth.

I have been visioning my future since I was a child. Sometimes we lose sight or sometimes our sights change.
I am visioning again, now.
what really matters.
in this 1 life of unknown.
I want to live happy
and I want those I love to live a happy life.

I want safe. To feel safe, secure, peaceful and more than comfortable---to be able to feel like I am thriving while just being.

Lena Ayala-Velasquez
October 15 · 21
Shared with Your friends

284

Happy birthday to me

♥ I am a Libra (10/15/88), year of the dragon

♥ I am into wearing my husband's clothes more than mine

♥ I love that we now get Angel every other week, since the pandemic

♥ For 7+ years I was teaching (infant/toddler, preschool, outdoor school, high-school substitute, child development for after school high-school)

♥ 3 of our kids are in school from home

♥ I am in training to become a certified life coach (Cycle of Courage Trained Practitioner: body mind soul)

♥ I am a doterra wellness advocate/consultant (I have a website link)

✦ I have been going to the chiropractor regularly since the pandemic (Feel Good Chiropractic and Live in Ease Chiropractic)

✦ I love being a part of soul care, mother's quest, freedom yoga (I am the ambassador for 3 months) and surrendered healing (Social Media Strategist and new member of the DreamTeam)

✦ I am currently in the shaklee prove it challenge

✦ I am still a member in BeachBod and today is the day I am setting to create routine

I am not a cake person but I do love cheesecake (homemade more)

I enjoy junk food more than candy and sweets

I'm not an ice cream person but I love frozen yogurt and if I do have ice cream, I like strawberry shortcake

gratitude saved me (I mean that, my whole life and will be a future book)

I choose Pepsi over coke, cream soda in a bottle over Pepsi and strawberry orchata most

I'm picky when it comes to meat

I enjoy bike riding, dirt bikes too, going on hikes and seeing new views

poetry slams are something I have never had enough of (attending) and would love in my life

I love salsas, hot sauce, spice

I have gotten married, twice!

I love wearing socks more than shoes

I love pillows, the bed is filled...the couches too

My favorite fruit might be plums

I enjoy mud runs

I love being on boats

I am terrified of heights (but love doing scary things)

I have my permit but need to practice driving and get my license one day I want to own my own home

I want to go to school for herbalism, child psychology, psychology, social work, mindfulness,

my heart beats for my family. I love being a mom of 4, a wife, a daughter, a sister, an Aunty and cousin and friend

I have desires of having a podcast, an email list, a website, finding my unique name (branding&logo), get yoga certified,

I am a self-published author of 2 books (one for sale and the other will be one day) and working to release another

April 3 · 21

Shared with Your friends

Our 3-year-old knows words like chiropractor and yoga.

They are in her vocabulary.

She goes with us, participates.

All four of our kids ages 14,13,9 and 3!

I say this with pride because at their ages this wasn't my reality. I am 32 and starting to really embrace this life.

They will get to open their minds and hearts a lot sooner.

We just spent 45 minutes in traffic. It wasn't frustrating because it meant extra angel time and it meant patience. There was a car on a flat, a young man falling asleep at the wheel. After so long, we were the only ones who made it a point to let him know. When we told him, he made his way to start pulling over. I keep thinking we were in the right place at the right time. I feel like we did something right.

What if someone would have seen my brother falling asleep before he got in his accident? What if this moment right now was something bigger than we could ever imagine?

Thankful grateful blessed ✧

What childhood traumas are you healing from? What are you giving your kids that you didn't have?

Lena Ayala-Velasquez
October 17, 2020 ·
Shared with Your friends
👥

I cannot believe the worrier in me has such a new calm.
this whole pandemic has given me a new peace, happiness, strength, courage, balance, faith and calm.
We have faced several sniffles, coughs, sneezes, snot, headaches, bug bites, pulled muscles, fears, during these 7months.
we have loved ones who had c19 last year and just learned confirmation. We have loved ones who passed away from c19 who had underlying health issues. We have loved ones who got c19 and beat it and are fine and some who now have to have breathing help because of it.
This scary and very real sickness has come close to home a few times.

The me before all this worried so much about everything. Does a sniffle or cough still concern me? yes. But I am more confident in my holistic learnings, I am more confident in our bodies, I am more confident in our faith and in our support systems, I am more at peace with everything. We have not been to a doctor's office in I don't know how long and only made a call once back in march, I think.

The worrier in me is more of a warrior these days. I am not upset at that. This phase of my life just is what it is.

When my dad's extra cologne spray broke and dint bring me to full tears, when Athena had a fever in march and I handled it with a different mindset, when loved ones shared they got sick and I was able to be positive, when we finally went to a couple of larger gatherings recently , when close relatives traveled different places and came around, with loved ones working in hospitals or in grocery stores and food places and more.......so many situations during this 7 month have shown me my growth and changes

I am not saying I am fearless; I am not saying my severe anxiety is all gone, I am not saying I do not have worries----because it all still exists. I still get the thoughts, sometimes more than other times, sometimes stronger than other times......
But I have been able to re-frame thoughts, I have been able to still be positive and remain in gratitude, I am learning to prioritize rest and sleep, I am forever learning/changing/growing.

I want the best for all my loved ones, all strangers, everyone. I want peace, happiness, health and wealth for all. I am really learning on healing myself first, in ways I have been needing to.

Today I am waking up. Thankful to be waking up. The past 2 nights I haven't been as great with my sleep- and although it was because of good reasons-no reason is "good enough."

I am so grateful for fresh air. For outside time, even if away from people by 6 feet or more. I am thankful for vitamins, herbs, emergenc orange juice boosters. I want to do all I can to be healthy before/during and after any sickness. I am thankful for chiropractic care. I am thankful to be exercising/working out and drinking more water and eating better lately. I am thankful for the peace of mind because I have always heard "stress is a killer"
I am thankful for my circle expanding in the ways to be in the presence of likeminded people who will help me learn and grow and be in community with. I am also grateful for those who aren't likeminded because I love learning from all. I am also thankful I am learning my boundaries and

what serves me/what doesn't. I am thankful for moments of yoga and meditation and really learning to breathe. I am thankful for it all. I hope to keep being thankful through it all.

It is hard to say who and how we will be in times of big worry, fear and experiences. It is hard to practice what you preach at times. It is different when something "happens to you." but is it? does it have to be? or can we learn to just be....to be confident and mindful and peaceful and calm.

I don't have all the answers. I know and hope everyone does what they feel is best for them and their families. Whether that is remote school, hybrid, flexible, homeschool. Whether that is going to work, not working, having to have childcare, having to get food stamps or unemployment or go to the food back. Whether that means sage the house, lighting candles, praying, wearing a mask, washing hands more than others, washing off groceries or not. Whether that means staying completely isolated or not. Whatever it means.
I hope whatever it means that you treat people with kindness and some understanding. I hope you

focus on your feelings/thoughts and growth. Lead by example. Find some peace.
There is too much hate and meanness in this world-especially when people do/believe different than others
There is too much judgement. Too much "I know better."

Be open to being taught and be brave to teach others. Be courageous to be you, to stand for what you believe and be open to knowing what works for you may not work for others. and that is ok.

We do have common stuff those. We need air, we need calm, we need happiness and laughter. We need support and love. We need water. We need sunlight and we need healing. not just the kind we seek when we are sick. We need healing on so many levels.
Everyone is fighting different battles, challenges, struggle, heartache and traumas.
We all have many layers and things happening in our worlds.
Please be respectful to those around you. even if our views are different. Everyone has a different

story and we do not know all the layers to each person we come across-we do not even know all the layers to those right next to us. So, I am learning to be mindful and accept people for who and where they are and with that-learning my boundaries and how I can support and be peaceful especially when I don't agree.

Hello Saturday. Praying for all, for whatever it is you are struggling with.
Hello surrender. It is ok to Speak up, it is ok to Speak out, it is ok to be Silent, it is ok to Sit with your feelings, it is ok to be ok and it is ok to not be ok.
Share your truths, share your knowledge, share your blessings, share your love.
have a blessed day
Lena Ayala-Velasquez
June 29 ·
Shared with Your friends

👥

I don't even remember the thoughts that lead to it...
but somehow, I was almost asleep last night then felt that urge to google things...

when my son was born, I had received some blood
results and information that lead to years later me
being in an office that treats people with cancer.
I was told I was ok and that chances of being in a
car accident and this coming about were likely the
same, not to worry unless anything changes (pains
or what not.)
To just continue living life.
well last night, I remembered this part of me. and I
started feeling tight in the chest, scared of death. I
haven't had that fear in a while, that level of
anxiety... but suddenly my sleep was scared away
and I wanted to cry and hold my kids and do
things different.
I felt like my world was crashing, and like I was
pretending things are good and better when they
aren't ...I started feeling like I was dying.... crazy
how moments of emotions and thoughts can make
you feel
or what they can make you realize.... true or not
I want to live life fullest and take risks and keep
working on being the healthiest version of myself.
I took the information and thought, maybe I need
a new checkup.
maybe I don't

They say there is no cure, but what if there is a cure---such as being mindful, change, being happy, chiropractic care, meditation, building community, engaging with family and all that good stuff
why do we need a diagnosis to push us to live life more fully?
why do we need a diagnosis to feel like we then have purpose or can help others?
I think of how I have lived to avoid the exact thing I may have.
I think of how unpredictable and uncertain life is, even when you try to get different outcomes
I also know that miracles are real and anything is possible
last night was tough
lead to some bad dreams
but I know no-matter what, I needed sleep and healthiest I need sleep
I know sleep is so important for healing and for accomplishing.
Hello Tuesday. Yoga felt different today.
I thought of what if the day comes that I physically can't
what if today helps that day not come at all

what if today is just today and tomorrow is
tomorrow and the days after, are what they are
but I enjoy right now
what if....
what is....

Who do you love to listen to? (Singer, Poet, Author, Podcast, Motivational speaker?) Who speaks to your soul, and why?

_____

_____

_____

_____

_____

_____

_____

_____

_____

_____

BODY MAINTENANCE

Lena Ayala-Velasquez
February 7, 2020 · Alameda ·
Shared with Your friends

It smells amazing here.

Enough toys for Athena to almost be completely entertained the whole hour.

a $37 Posture Analysis, Neuro Exam & Chiro Consult at Feel Good Chiropractic.

Investing in your health is so hard to do when others things always feel more important.

But I always remind myself I can't be the best me or help the people I love best until I help myself.

July 7, 2020 · Alameda ·

Shared with Your friends

Today is another first day of the rest of my life.

My new story, my new journey.

For years I have been dealing with grief, mindset change, personal growth and self-care.

Today is another step in the right direction.

I can feel it.
Everything I am doing is in alignment.

I walked in ready, in pain, super tense, scared.
Leaving feeling relief, emotional (happy), lighter,
that I made the right choice.

It was meant to be.

This is a big commitment and it takes a village but
I am so thankful for my village and my growth and
my today.

I see people leaving and coming happy here. Her
name is Heidi which is the name of someone I
love. She has been practicing for 15 years which is
my special number.
I was able to afford it, unexpectedly. And not.
This is my new life, my new story.

Self-care is not selfish and should not make you
feel guilty.

Oxygen mask on you first so you can help others
🖤

I'm growing, I'm changing, I'm leading by my truth and example and I feel so proud, excited and at peace 💕

October 9, 2020 ·

Shared with Your friends

👥

In February I ran across a deal on social media to see a chiropractor. It landed me in Alameda with a woman name Heidi for a consultation.

She recommended to get x-rays done which I did March 12, right at the beginning of the pandemic. June 26, I finally made it back in her office for the follow up visit to talk about the x-rays and next steps.

I knew what to expect "horrible news and not being able to afford it."

The story of my life. Insurance never covers this stuff. Insurance only will offer me pain medicines I won't use and physical therapy that only does so much for me.

She told me I had Osteoarthritis, stage 2 going on 3. Stage 4 being untreatable but right now she could help. She told me my neck was the worst of the x-rays and this could explain the constant headaches I have been complaining about for years, the unable to sleep for years, the severe anxiety. Heidi told me a year of support for tissue fibrosis is what she was recommending 3 times a week for 3 months- to slow it down significantly, not to fix what has been taking place my whole life. I was told I have a reversed cervical curve which is a longer process to treat. With all this news, Heidi still said she believed I would be feeling significantly better at the end of the 3 months.

I knew it would all come down to money. I have always wanted help but couldn't afford it. I knew I wanted to try, that's why I was there. I knew I wasn't going to hear great news or get a handout or find help for free. I am willing to show up, however many times, however long. I am willing to put in the work.... but I can't put in the money I don't have.

I have heard it all before. I have seen a chiropractor before twice for adjustments (full body I think in 2015.) I have seen massage therapists and the doctor and they all say the same-that my back is very messed up for someone my age. I have tried heated pillows, different pillows, back cracks, essential oils, so many things for pain and help. I even tried acupuncture at the end of last year.

Heidi told me the cost for her help. The cost of more than my rent but with an upfront payment I could get a discount for a little less than my rent amount.

All of the coaching I have been getting, all of the courses and support I have been taking has led me here. That a way will be found, money is everywhere.
I had the mindset of I am going to make this happen. I want to. My mindset was "I already know what not trying this looks like. I need to know what trying this could be." My new mindset was I deserve this. I should have done it sooner but the time I know, why wait anymore. This happened in a point in my life where I am learning and taking self-care more seriously, I am investing in me and making life worth living.

It wasn't that easy. The thoughts of "I have gone this long just fine, I can go longer." The thought of

"I can think of other things to spend $20 on let alone the cost of rent." The thoughts of other things are more important and if I do this its taking away from my family. The thoughts of how can I get this money when we barely afford rent as it is. Would it be worth it? What if I come out worse than I went in?

But I changed each of those thoughts to the opposite and I told myself "If this was the car needing fixing, we'd have to make it happen. This body is my car and I am just as important and worth it. I have to make me a priority."

I loved the location in Alameda. I loved that this person's name was Heidi (we love a woman named Heidi). She has been working in this for 15 years which is my favorite number. She has the same birthday as our oldest child.

No, it's no coincidence. It's meant to be. (Oh, and in our time together I myself joined beachbod fitness and when in conversation with her, she also was a member! I had never heard of this before or knew anyone who was a member!) Tell me this isn't alignment?

Between that time in her office June 26 and talking for days after.... I was in her office July 7 for my first adjustment!
yes, that means I got the money and paid and started treatment this year. I say treatment. We had some hard financial situations happen which led to some temporary loans and we made the choice to pay with money that wasn't exactly ours, that now all these months later we have to pay back. I share this because I am not overwhelmed. I believe everything happens for a reason. I believe everything happened how it was supposed to and I was finally in the right space in life to make this happen and accept it and go for it and want it bad enough and trust it finally.

July 7, I had my first adjustment and this upcoming Tuesday will be my last for this timeframe. The total of 36 adjustments over 3 months. I also was given tools for spinal movement to do at home, exercises to do and a re-eval which happened earlier this week. Adjustments were quick. Sometimes just in and out within like 5 minutes. Yes, my whole family would say "you are paying too much for a couple of minutes." Yes, I too had my doubts and questions and concerns. But nobody could tell me how I feel. Almost every single time I left her office, I left glowing. I felt great. Sometimes my neck wouldn't crack and I would think "is it not working, oh no I paid and didn't get a result." But in reality- There are always results.

*I fix my posture more
*I have more energy
*I have less anxiety
*I once I went in with a horrible headache and left without it
*My daughter joined me once and now wants to go
*My husband joined me once and this whole process and journey has made a believer out of him.
He notices the changes more "she doesn't ask me to massage her anymore. She used to ask me every day. many times, a day. she would be in constant pain. She would complain."
*I started working out. Which use to hurt me tremendously and scare me so much I wouldn't try. I would cry tears in yoga! so yes, I am more flexible

*Heidi asked my daughter does she notice a difference in me and iris replied "big difference"
*I look forward to our visits. I look forward to getting adjusted. I look forward to conversating and being in her positive energy and having her encouragement and support
*I don't crack my neck or back myself like I use to for relief.

Just recently we went over my posture pictures from February 7 and October 6. My husband and I could clearly see the difference.
Heidi reminded me of the notes from the first day I came in, my story, my goals and we sat and talked about how I feel these days and my goals now. I will never feel like I am 100% but I feel like we made such huge improvements with how I feel.
She didn't order new x-rays because it won't show I am fixed but it will show change.

and I know it to be true. I know how I feel, I know what I see, I am keeping a journal of this journey.

I am so thankful. I am thankful for all of the connections, the coaching, the investment in myself, the support, the love, the encouragement. I am thankful I tried. I do not feel "healed" but I do feel so connections, so much better and I am healing constantly.

I feel like I made the right choice. I will always wish it was cheaper and wish it was easier to find such care. So many could benefit from this amazing care.

I want to continue. I will have to figure out how I can. But I am so thankful I tried this, I am thankful for how this has gone for me, I am thankful for it all.

I look forward to my next last day and who knows what the future holds but I see getting adjusted as becoming a part of my "normal." I want to see monthly massages as my new normal and yoga/exercise/coaching/holistic healing/herbalism/better nutrition/better sleep........

I will say this has been worth it.

When you don't think of money as the all-time barrier. When you don't let the negative thoughts rule, your decision making.
It all makes such a difference.

I believe everything I am doing and have been doing, all plays a part in how I am feeling these days. But I can't deny how different I have felt physically since I started chiropractic care

With Dr. Heidi Wroebel at Feel Good Chiropractic

I just recently started following her on ig and fb and I love all of the inspiration, motivation and positivity
6/29/20 what if I pay a chiropractor and get hurt worse?
 What if I feel like my money is wasted? We can travel with that money instead. It's the cost of rent. No one can promise me it will be worth it. All other dreams can still be possible, but with a healthier and happier me if I go to chiropractor. It's what I haven't tried. I know what it's like without it. What if I feel better? What if my discomfort and pain start to leave? If the car

needed to be fixed, we would find a way. I am the car right now and I am just as important. Oxygen mask on me first.

Trust in your higher power, your new story, all you are learning, in all you know to be real, in what you feel, in the unknown, in abundance, in meant to be.
The more you give, the more you get.
August 25, 2020 ·
10 days without seeing my chiropractor, she was on vacation.
Vacation, time off is so important for any and every one and I think everyone needs to take care of themselves.
Especially when we are "depending" on people to help us with our self-care, yeah-we need those people taking care of us to take care of themselves first.
The last time I was here I had woken up in pain that lasted for a couple of days.
Today I am not in that pain.
I have done some stretching throughout these days and a tiny self-adjusting but nothing compared to what I use to do, daily!
I have already come far mentally and physically.

today I got my spinal hygiene movement backpack
some stretches to do, 3-minute laying on this
back/neck rollers and watch out for flare ups.
starting small but goal to get to 20minutes a day.

again, another 2st day of the rest of my life.
new step in this new journey.

I'm doing it! it does feel good.

I told her I signed up for this fitness thing last
night and she said to just listen to my body, don't
do too much too fast but that it should be ok

it's all coming together, all in its time — at Feel
Good Chiropractic.
Lena Ayala-Velasquez
October 26, 2020 ·
It has been 13 days since my last adjustment.
Since then, I have been feeling some stress and
anxiety here and there.

Since then, I have wondered "will I start cracking
my own back and neck for relief? will I need relief
soon? Why isn't anything bothering me? when will

I have to ask my husband for a massage? How long can I last until I feel like I need to see the chiropractor?"

I also had the thoughts of "I don't want to remember what it felt like to be in pain, to feel hopeless and hope chiropractic help can work" "I am enjoying feeling good, I want to stay enjoying feeling good. This means I need to get back in for weekly adjustments"

Today is day 1 for my next journey. My next journey of once-a-week adjustments.

Just months before, I was seeing Dr. Heidi 3 times a week (for my first ever real investment and help with a chiropractor.)

I had seen a chiropractor twice before, in my whole life and loved the relief it gave me for--that few days. I couldn't afford to do anything more. It was a gift at that time. Nothing ever seemed to heal me.
So, this time I invested in real help, real support, a real plan.

Dr. Heidi has helped change my life, for the better. I love speaking with her. I love her care. I love her positive social media posts. I love her office vibes. I love her energy, her honesty, her values and beliefs. I love getting to know her.
and I love how I feel when I leave her office, physically.

Today I went in feeling good. Not sure if I needed to invest to continue to get help.
In reality I knew I needed to be here; I knew I could only benefit.
Right when I laid down, I could feel it in my body "there is still work to be done"
when everything was done, I felt relief I didn't know I needed....
I felt happier, I felt confident in my decision to continue, I felt a boost of energy and courage.

thank you to my husband for this birthday gift.
thank you to myself for this birthday gift.
thank you, Dr. Heidi, for your gifts.

I can't wait to one day have my children adjusted, and my husband.
October 26, 2020 ·

Yes, I would recommend feel good Chiropractic.
Every time I step into this office I am always
reminded of how much good people and places
matter to me
Dr. Heidi and I get to chat some days more than
others and I always leave with a smile.
She has such a welcoming environment; she has
such a positive and loving energy.
From the day we first met, she said she was proud
of me for taking the step to be there.
she has championed me every step of the way,
and not in a "sales pitch kind of way"
whether I had paid already or not yet-she has
always been supportive.
She is extremely knowledgeable. I can tell by how
she speaks, by how she is with me, by how people
are always coming and going.
I always enter and leave knowing-this connection
was no coincidence and I am always so grateful
for it.
November 12, 2020 ·
I purposely scheduled my chiropractic
appointments for Thursdays. For the simple fact
that I wanted to get adjusted on THANKFUL
THURSDAY.

Today has been so valuable. I used to crack my knuckles, my back, my neck a lot. On my own. self-relief, self-adjustments to help with the discomfort and pain.

Today I am reminded, this investment in myself is no longer just CRACKS in the office (this treatment is the fine dining, the level up) the proper wording is adjustments.

It felt so wonderful to get adjusted today. To start my morning and day off with that self-care and that morning time with Heidi.

I love that social media has given us both the opportunity to get to know each other more, give us more to talk about and connect with.

Today felt much needed.

I was reminded last week as I went down a big slide with Athena, fear of pain made me frantic and I actually hurt my lower back a bit. The pain and discomfort didn't last long. I was reminded with that experience of my life before chiropractic care. I used to be scare to make simple movements (lay on my stomach, cry through yoga, workout) These days I don't hesitate like I used to, I don't feel the way I used to, I don't cry through yoga. The stretch now feels like challenge and not pain.

I have come so far with all of the choices and progress and growth in my life.

Today my neck and upper back felt so great to get relief. I feel like a towel full of water that got rung out. My adjustments were much needed and I left feeling re-charged and ready to take on the day even better.

November 19, 2020 ·

Thankful Thursday all the way

*I went to the chiropractor today and I was feeling it in my body that I was excited and couldn't wait to feel better.

Unexpectedly and to my surprise I was on the wall as November start of the month. How cool is that. My story up there on the wall, my pictures. My journey being shared. along with others. I have read about others on the wall but it never clicked in my mind "star of the month" There is something about leaving that office, feeling like a better me. It's not just the chiropractic care and adjustments. It's the conversation, the smell, the feel of the environment.

I was so excited to share with my family.

My uncle says "of course she has to put you on the wall because to make you feel special so you keep paying. To make it feel like 5 minutes of work is worth your money"

what I told him is "you don't know how I feel, how I feel now compared to months and years before, How I feel when I leave that office after getting adjusted. "
You cannot make everyone understand.

But here I am, someone who believes that $20 is expensive but yet I invested in this! twice! That's how much I feel and believe in it. That's what it means to me!
 I borrowed, we put off other things, I used all resources to make this real for me. For too long I couldn't afford it, other things were more important.
would I still rather use my money for a vacation or something? yes.
But now I can enjoy a vacation, or a regular day without the constant pain I was in.

not everyone will understand. and that is ok.

It took me a long time to get to where I am today
as well.
I don't need everyone to understand.

I just need to make it to my appointments. Do my
at home care. Continue making myself the best
version of me I can.

Look up chiropractic care. All of the benefits are
amazing.
I feel like I can't go wrong with it.
and while it's paid for, invested in, enjoyed----I am
going to love every bit of it and get the most I can
from my experiences.

Before this I would ask my husband to massage
me, many times daily. I only just recently asked
him this past week when I was having some neck
pain from pulling something stretching.
that is a huge deal!
that is big progress.
that is not coincidence!

I am so thankful for the help I am getting, the care
I have found, the new opportunities in alignment
with me because of the choices I am making.

This post wasn't going to be just on my visit today, but it is now.

thankful, grateful, blessed
December 21, 2020 ·
I am thankful to be here this morning with my husband.
Monday's matter, mental health matters, mornings matter
My husband came here just a few days ago on thankful Thursday for his first ever exam, report find and treatment all for $21 (it was a deal we ran across) He had a great experience and thanks to someone out there he was able to sign up and pay for his care package which is 7 more visits and so here we are to start our Monday.
This time I came with him because I wanted to hear about what's going on with him, I wanted to meet the person, I wanted to support my husband who was nervous and excited.
I loved hearing from my husband how since his adjustments, that he noticed he's sleeping in longer (up at 6 instead of 5) and trust me when I say that is huge for him! He talked about

foot/ankle pain he has had for a while now and the chiropractor worked on it right away.

I believe we were there for a good hour. he was worked on in many forms, his first experience was I believe about 45 minutes and they will get shorter. I am just thankful to Dr. Bryan for taking the time to talk so much with us, answer questions, take time to get to know each other, and for all of the time he put into helping my husband on his journey.

I am thankful my husband has this journey for himself. I am so thankful everything worked out financially. I am so thankful he feels like he is in good hands and that the timing and everything for him feels like such a match.

I am excited that my husband and I both started chiropractic journeys this year and that we are both invested in our healing and growth. I am thankful we can have conversations and understand each other more, differently and in this new context. I am thankful this is a part of our life now.

Sometimes things feel too good to be true and your brain tells you to wait for/beware of the scam and the downfall. But I am learning and working on trust. I am learning and working on the goodness.

It felt so awesome to hear language used, that now doesn't sound foreign to me. It feels amazing to be able to have conversations with more understanding and also still so many questions.

I feel like when you explore new people and places-it's so easy to have doubt, fears, unsure trust and you want to feel people out. I think that is normal.

when you make changes. You start to learn and experience what is possible. You learn by doing. You learn by trying. You grow from these moments in life.

I found myself breathing along with my husband, even though he was getting the work done and I was just watching. I wanted to document this journey for him.

I am that much more ready and excited to see my chiropractor this week.

I am that much more ready and excited to prioritize sleep, exercise, meditation, yoga, eating better, family time, self-care and just to live healthier lives.

I am thankful my husband gets to start off his day and week this way. I am so thankful we get to start our day and week this way.

Monday motivation

Monday's matter!

mental-health matters

Mornings matter

and I am loving how it's going so far. I felt so energized I went on a short run. I love this feeling of feeling better, feeling nourished, feeling fueled and enlightened and accomplished.

January 7

Ever since getting sick in December, I felt like I was kind of setback. I need to change my story...It's true I have been in so much pain (back pain, neck ---even leg.) But I am so grateful to have paid for chiropractic care last year! I am so thankful for this journey and for Dr. Heidi.

I am thankful that for this new year I finished my 9th visit out of 20. I am thankful I still have more than half left to look forward to.

When I first started this journey, I was in this office 3 times a week. It made a huge difference! Now I go once a week, I can feel the shift in my body from not going as often. But I also know my

mind body and soul are so much stronger now
than a year ago.
Every time I enter this office I look forward to
positive conversations and amazing care. Every
time I leave this office, I leave empowered and
feeling amazing. These last few times I still leave
with some noticeable pain still there, but I leave so
much better than I entered!
I think one day I would love to work at that front
desk, I think My new story always wants
chiropractic care in my life and in my family's life.
I am so thankful I found this space and place when
I did. Timing was everything. Everything aligned.
I am thankful for my adjustments today (to my
back, my neck, my foot/ankle....) My body feels so
much better.
Then I get home and the work continues! It has to.
I have a whole lifetime of habits to change, stories
to change, mindset to shift, new routines to create
and progress to make.
Life-long learner. Healing takes time and work.
I am so grateful for it all.
6/29/20
What I really want is not fb – it's a blog. It's a
podcast, to write book sand to coach.
March 3 21

Shared with Your friends

👥

I look forward to my weekly adjustments and time with Dr. Heidi.
For a period of time, I was coming in 3 times a week.
Now, today -I learned I am graduating to twice a month.
I have 4 visits left in my paid plan. Which means two visits this month, well, 1 more now. and two visits next month.

That for me, mentally was a lot to process.
Because sometimes I feel like I am barley making it through the week without her.

With a month of doing yoga, I do feel better.
With giving up meat and soda, I do feel better.
with several coaches in my life to help me mentally, emotionally, spiritually-I do feel in a better space of taking care of me.
With all I have invested into chiropractic care, I feel and know I am in a way different place than when I started last year.

I am actually able to do yoga and workout now, without crying from pain. I am able to move more, I am working on my posture more and so is my whole family.

The news of coming twice a week and only 3 visits left can be overwhelming.
Really, with barley making rent this month, I can't even entertain the thought of putting down money for 20 more adjustments.
I know I am not fully healed. I also know I can make anything happen. I know chiropractic Care will stay in my life and tool box.
I know I have to process the reality of things, the emotions and thoughts and then get back to the doing what serves me and creating the life I love.

I feel so great leaving the office. It's amazing how everything connects, how finding the right person and place matters.

I am so thankful for this journey.
April 28 · 21
Shared with Your friends

Today was the last day of my second care plan (20 adjustments + a re-evaluation)

Right when I walked in to wait, I always read the whiteboard and the "chalkboard" to see what quotes are up.
While reading I see prizes for a raffle and then I look over at the "wall" and get excited because there is a May Raffle.
I know I won a raffle prize last October, A blender that my whole family loves. I get the thoughts "it would be selfish to try and even want to win again"
"Winning again, can't be in alignment for me, it doesn't work that way"
"I am grateful for all I have"
"But, these 3 prizes are amazing! exactly what I need/want. I deserve it. I would write a review, just to do it anyways. Why not try, it can't hurt. Go for it"
"Tea time with Heidi or a 60minute massage" are the kinds of self-care and journey I am on in life.

anyways, back to today's appointment.
Dr. Heidi shared with me when I first came in, my consultation and my two evaluations.

I was blown away!
That girl from February, June, October----woah.
That isn't my story anymore.
I am not in pain every single day. I reached my
goals and continue to improve.
I continue to have new goals.
I know that I want adjustments and chiropractic
care to continue.
For me, it's been so worth it. I don't want to "not
have it"
I know I feel better with this care in my life.
The fact that I used to come 3 times a week and
am now considering once a month (the fact that I
can even say that without anxiety now, is
amazing!)
I am not completely healed but man, I am not that
girl from before.

Before, I "couldn't afford this"
before, I couldn't do yoga or workout without
crying from the back/neck pain
before, I was a different me.
before, I just wanted to be happier, feel better,
feel more energized and get better sleep. Back
and neck pain was really traumatizing for me.

I am so thankful for Dr. Heidi.
she is gentle, patient, she cares deeply, her space
is welcoming and motivating, I love getting to
know her as a person. I feel more powerful,
healthier and confident by having her support in
my life.

and, my daughter may be next in having care here.
I feel that confident and thankful.

*****I share all of these posts and reflections
because even as I sit here writing this now. I am in
pain. It is December 2021. I haven't been seeing
Dr. Heidi the way I was. I have been blessed to
see a chiropractor, Dr. Bryan up until November,
with my husband. We both would get adjusted
together, it was a little more affordable and
different styles of care.
It has been some time out of the office. Scarcity
mindset, reality and all those old stories have
crept back in.
I have been in horrible pain, to where some days I
stayed in bed scared to participate in yoga- even
though I know I feel better once I get on my mat.

I have felt like I went back to where I was two years ago and like I messed all of my healing and progress up.
But while looking back, I know the truth. I can change my story.
And someone told me recently that "effort is never wasted"

We are human. Sometimes we feel like we go backwards, but you can never truly go backwards because you have already gone forward.
It is ok to be human.

I have plans to go back to Dr. Heidi. I have plans to continue chiropractic care.

This book has many different sections of people, places, and spaces that bring me to different self-care, but truth is- everything is connected. Every piece is a piece of me and it all works together.

DOTERRA

January 1, 2019 ·
Doterra essential oils in the diffuser, warm bottles and chamomile tea, baby rub, bathroom with hot water for steam+ diffuser, hugs, sleep...

she sounds better with All this but she's not better.

Her voice isn't hers; you can hear the sickness. No fever or snot or anything. She's drinking fine. She's even playing.

Definitely napping easier and more which is not like her.

Doctors' office is closed.

Emergency room is better safe than sorry, I also don't want to put her through distress and more discomfort and make her worse if she's getting better.

We don't get parent handbooks; we just have our gut instincts and whatever knowledge/education/experience.

We have loved ones, opinions, their knowledge/education and experiences.

Gotta pray in the end you did the right thing and the best thing.

Google will have you diagnosed with everything and put so much extra stress on your brain/spirit/health.

Angel is gone, my husband got called in early, it's the first day of the new year and life is teaching us, testing us and blessing us in ways we don't fully see and do see.

Time to buy a humidifier. We should own one of those regardless.

July 8, 2020 ·

When you realize your two-year-old emptied much of your doterra oregeno oil 😭😭😭😭

It's expensive

We have used it often and much of it

There's still some left

Eventually we can buy more

*at least she was doing it because she has seen me do it often.

She is learning

She wasn't just emptying

But man, it's strong, "wasted", my fault for leaving it down low

Can't wait for our new furniture to get here so we can set up/create the room of vision ✨💀🩶

Have you ever been angry at someone? Are you able to realize the role you could play? Can you see from a different perspective?

September 16, 2020 ·

A great reason to have great sleep, or good enough sleep...

For mornings when you are up before 5am and your toddler is sneezy and snotty.

Thank you doterra essential oils: for bottoms of feet and for the diffuser. Baby chest rub, orange juice, mommy cuddles, tissue and immune support, elevated pillows.

Yes, I have all the thoughts from negative to more positive.

"What's going on"

"Is she getting sick? Dumb question"

"Who's been around? Who were they around"?

"Window was open, yay I put footsie pajamas on her last night"

"It's been Smokey and wonky weather "

"We have all we need"

"She's gotten sick before during this 6 month and we've managed "

"This too shall pass"

"Always praying for no Covid"

"What can I do better to get her to eat better so it'll support her"

"Sleep will help"

"Doctors office is close by; thankful we haven't had to go in very long time"

"Wish my husband wasn't leaving for work this early"

"Bodies are made for this"

Let's get back to bed 🖤✨

Hello Wednesday.
Welcoming it all as it is, as it comes.
Praying for missing people to be found. I can't get
these souls off my mind.
October 28, 2020 ·
So often we talk about things that are bad or
really good, because that is what is present for us.
Bad and good situations are the present feelings
and thoughts.
sometimes we forget the in-between.

I am so thankful the past however many nights
Athena hasn't woken up with any new bites.
We have been keeping footsie pajamas on her
we have been closing the windows at night
my husband looks for and kills and mosquitos-
those baby ones are really small
we had taken the plants out of our room
we bought a citronella candle that sits on the
dresser and has yet to be lit
we use the doterra blend my cousin brought us
"terrashield" and rub it on Athena's face and hands
whatever skin is showing (at night)
we put the diffuser on
we have our ultrasonic plug ins
lavender Epsom baths

When I stop and think of how frustrated I would
be to wake up to new bites, to scary bites-I have
to take the time to show how grateful I am for all
of the recent days we haven't woken up to that

old bites are healing
scars are healing
we have been using "Emu Joy -on the go stick-
portable relief" from amazon for the itching and
healing process

as I was writing this, the screen for my daughter's
window came, yay. she loves her window and
fresh air and cold

*Sometimes things feel good
sometimes they feel bad

but let's not forget about the space in-between,
what that means and how that feels
April 8, 2020 ·
I woke up around 3:30unable to sleep, for a long
time.

I started thinking if I get sick, if I were to catch this covid 19 or sick at all at this time- what that would mean.
How things would change again.
How scary it would be.
How hard it would be as the one home caring for our kids.
How do you quarantine in your own home?

Some of those are easy to know answers and some not.

I thought of the so many people who have already had to live a version of this.

The sad stories keep it real. The recovery stories keep it all feeling manageable.
None of them -an easy normal.

Now I'm up at 6 and hard to sleep again.

We have two family members in and out for work. I have read these next couple of weeks will be the hardest and have large numbers of people dying. That is scary. I want my husband and brother home instead of working. I want my uncle home instead of our and about. I want no visitors. I want the time to really lockdown- be safe, flatten the curve and truly get to know what really matters to each of us.

I also don't want to live in fear.

I have my diffuser going: doterra oils:
frankincense, on guard, melaleuca.
Thankful for that investment I made years ago.

Nights and mornings are really cold without a house heater.
Thank goodness for all of our blankets and beds and couches and pillows.
November 13, 2020 ·
Last night I went to bed with physical pain in my throat, as if I pulled something. Not a sore throat like sickness inside.
I used the heated lavender turtle, I put on the doterra diffuser and I went to bed with 1 more person added to secret Santa online
great blessings to weigh out the negativity

*This morning I decided I will have tea and for the first time I will use a piece of honeycomb from our great neighbor carl. Its waxy but I heard and read you can eat it. Cheers to new experiences.

my goal is to do things today that will bring me peace and happiness and better health.

his act of kindness is my blessing and I am using it, no longer letting it sit.

*I woke up to mom my sent me a picture of her at the age 16(that someone sent to her). I am happy she wanted to share that with me

*I rolled on my "now and zen" from pure romance and got started on my 36-minute workout through BEACHBODY on demand. today is day 19 full body burn

"It is a good day to have a good day"
Hello Fri-yay
faith over fear
flowing not forcing
feel the feelings
feel it to heal it
faith it till you make it

things that make me feel good are based on the moment but what has been consistent is (rest, brushing teeth, essential oil rolls on, essential oils, diffuser, creating the spaces I enjoy to look at and be in, getting rid of clutter, getting things done, grace/guilt and gratitude)

I haven't opened our bedroom window in a while due to the cold but I did today and I am loving the fresh cool air coming through. It feels awakening, it feels refreshing, it feels clean and it feels right. Gratitude saved my life; it made my life and it helps me live to the fullest

Lena Ayala-Velasquez

March 30, 2020 ·

what a month it has been.

march madness for sure.

blessings in disguise, definitely.

we officially moved back into our old house in alameda on the 1st, after exactly a year away (in San Leandro)

my niece and her kids were here for 16 days so unpacking didn't get done while she was here because we were out every day all day-except the last 5 days she was here.

then the day she left was shelter in place. so, all to say we are on day 30 of the month and lots of

unpacking still to be done. we can't shop or hunt
for dressers and things we need because
everything is closed and we have to stay indoors.
so, unpacking still can't be done because we need
certain things in order to empty boxes and them
to find their places.
this house isn't like it was before, less counter
space and shelves gone and stuff. this house isn't
like San Leandro with closets and too many
cupboards.
but what a blessing to be home, especially during
a pandemic.
Athena had a fever for a few days and stores were
out of medicine. oregano and coconut oil saved
us. Pedialyte has been great, along with our
doterra oils and diffuser.
this month many birthdays were celebrated in
quarantine and some got cancelled.
this month my husband lost hours at work-lost his
Saturday job, my chiropractor visit couldn't
happen, schools for all kids were closed down,
angel regular weekends were changed.
this month I was able to get fake nails for the first
time in like 6 years, got my haircut after more than
2 years, dyed my hair with a box dye, got the
deposit back from the other house, voted, got x-

rays done for chiropractor, my oldest brother
came to visit.
we have played board games we never opened,
read new books, watched movies and new shows
as a family. we have stayed home and enjoyed all
it has to offer.
iris is still in the process of transitioning to
alameda school from San Leandro.
this month we saw angel 6 days, tomorrow will be
7 (even if 1 day just meant dropping him off in the
morning)
my family lost a family member due to covid 19
this month has been very challenging and full of
blessings.
thankful through it all. flowing, not forcing.
surrender not fighting.

*******In 2020 I decided to take Doterra training
to become a dōTERRA® Essential Oil Specialist
and I got my Certification before the year ended.

CAROLINA AYALA

Independent Wellness Advocate
I have been attracted to essential oils before I
knew to learn about them. In 2014 my cousin
came to me about Doterra and I have been using

them ever since. Finally in 2020 I am ready to advocate.

I share these posts and reflections, not to try to sell anything to anyone. Not to try to make believers out of anyone. Doterra just happens to be a part of my journey, healing and story.

I share my true "diary" in case it helps others reflect. In case it matters, beyond me.

MINDFUL WRITING 5-day CHALLENGE BY NADIA COLBURN

DAY 1
We have a meditation, a reading and then a prompt-then time to write

Prompt: imagine you are a doorway.
What do you want to enter?

SAFE HAVEN

A few small stones can be so many things
Iris is my daughter
Iris is in our eyes

I want to be a safe haven
So, any and all may be welcome
And most will feel safe enough to do so
I want to know when any alarms should go off to
help me protect all that is sacred and important
Weeds, stones, vacant, occupied
All is as it should be
I welcome it all

I want peace, happiness, joy, love and utopia to enter/be
5/24/21

Prompt: I speak for

I SPEAK FOR...

I speak for me

The me who is shy and scared
The me who can see myself in others
I speak for me
Knowing it helps me become free from my own fears and judgements
I speak for me
Knowing I am never alone
Someone out there knows
Do I want to be known?
I just want to serve
Offer my story and honesty as support
I speak for me
When someone sees something in me and asks me to speak
To use my voice, because it matters
That is when I answer

Its still for me, it's an honor to say yes- to share
my journey
I speak for me
With integrity

I speak for...

Children, who I see are not being heard
For their clear shared words
I am just a mirror, of that child inside of me
That mother who is me, that teacher I want to be
That adult that will be heard and taken more
seriously

I speak for, my body
Only I know my pain and suffering
Only I can speak for the challenges and what feels
helpful
5/25/21

Prompt: imagine writing from the love window
Words you can use: window, kiss, want, shell,
face, language

WINDOW OF LOVE

My love window is wide and tall

Open to loving all who it can connect with
In love and loving can differ
But what is the difference?

I love opening the windows in the morning
Opening the curtains to allow all the light and air
to flow through
Natural lights, save electricity
No longer in, hiding
Of the outside world
Of the cold or hot weather
It works- for all temperatures
I open the door as well, but I appreciate the
screens
However, our back door has no screen
No screen allows bugs and children to come and
go

To dream is to open the love window
We never know what or who will come and go
Someone from the past
Someone no longer here
Sometimes the unexplainable, even the fears
5/26/21

Day 4. Today I did this practice in the afternoon
instead of the morning.
This writing challenge, freedom yoga, open-source
wellness, meditation and my inner being
It's all connected and connecting
It all flows

Prompt 'don't go off somewhere else"
Words you can use: ground, strong, nobody, own,
name, traveler, lope, rope

SOMEWHERE ELSE

Don't go off somewhere else
Unless that's where you want to be
Is it where you want to go?
Ground yourself in your truth
Be strong in your morals, truth and values
Nobody else can live your life for you
Travel and be a traveler
This is your journey
Your story
You hold the rope
Does it hurt?
Do you need to let it go?
Why are you holding on?
5/27/21

Day 5, last day of the challenge

Prompt: I am offering this...
Words you can use: socks, corn, knocking,
treasure, outside, remember

I AM OFFERING...

I am offering this
Permission for me to be me
Me to be enough
Perfect enough, as is
Wise enough to choose for myself
To believe in myself and trust me

I am offering this of me
To help you do the same for yourself
And in return for me, as well
5/28/21

Boundaries
I am strong. I hold boundaries.
I can't always control who and what enters
But if I could, I would allow peace
And honesty
I know honesty isn't always peaceful

I will allow whole people

I want joy and laughter to enter.
I want beautiful and therapeutic smells
I want calm to enter
I want chill, playful and restoration

I want equality, freedom, justice, safety, comfort, and smiles

I want visitors to want to stay awhile
9/12/20

I SPEAK FOR

I speak for the voice inside that is scared to speak up
For my inner child that now knows more than enough

I speak for the children who confide in me
I speak for the situations that need more publicity

I speak for my future, so I document it all
I speak for my past, that's why I write it all

I speak for my heart; I know it needs to be heard

I speak for.........

What do you speak for?
Who do you speak for?
Do you want to speak more?
Do you feel heard?

Why do you speak?
Why are you afraid of an audience when they are
who you seek?

Do you need an audience?
....I speak for me
9/13/20

August 20, 2020 ·
Shared with Your friends

👥

Reflecting on summer on this Thankful Thursday
Day
*As Iris is on day 2 of school, Angel on day 3 and
Leo starting next Thursday- I know that means our
summer has "ended"
*Angel left Monday and that usually means back
to school and only seeing him Friday afterschool-

Sunday morning. But we are hopeful distance learning means more Angel time

Summer went by fast. I can't believe how fast. As march came and the pandemic happened, we started getting angel for two weeks on and two weeks off. Then as summer came, we would see him 1 week on and 1 week off. This all a huge blessing for our family for so many reasons why. we thought with the pandemic we wouldn't be able to do anything, not how we once planned or hoped

but summer was amazing for so many reasons why

*This summer came a little earlier. school ended earlier

*I started seeing a chiropractor

*I was a part of mother's quest summer series

*I joined cycle of courage with Jessica stong

*I joined a week of overcoming overwhelm with Jennifer White

*I participated in the mommy and me challenge with Cayla Craft

*We celebrated many birthdays, even a proposal

*My niece syahra came and we saw the kids

*Iris had her first sleepover at a friend's house

*We took our first family trip to Tahoe, with a stop in Sacramento to ride down with our Houser family
*We took a trip to visit my brother and family in Santa margarita
*We enjoyed hikes and bike rides and family and life
*My husband took some time off, with pay
we took two trips for two-night stays!
taking trips is our goals, taking time off is our goals, staying two nights instead of 1
this was huge for our family, it meant so much, both times we saw/experienced these trips with family
these trips gave us new views and new experiences and feelings of fulfillment, restoration and happiness
we got the house together a lot more in several ways
I feel so great that the pandemic didn't hold us hostage and that we still have dreams and goals of more
so much more filled our everyday summer days
but these highlights really filled my cup
so thankful for all of the moments, the faith, our time together

Lena Velasquez
August 13, 2020 ·

Shared with Your friends and Julie's friends

👥

Today I went on my Virtual Milestone Hike with
Julie Lieberman Neale.
You may have heard me talk about her before. She
has been in my life since high school but over
these past several years she has been a constant
in my life.
I am constantly inspired, supported and motivated
by her.
The work she does in this world is so valuable,
necessary and sometimes overlooked.
I have participated in many groups Julie has
facilitated, in person and virtual.
I have invested my time and money...she has
invested her time, money, knowledge, heart,
resources, guidance and so much more.

During this time today it was just her and I. Two of
my children walked in (and during like the "worst"
of times when I am deep in my hike with my eyes
closed) and so I was distracted a bit but I decided
for the first time to announce I was closing my

door. Then I closed my door to my room. I immediately thought "I could've handled that better. if I just gave them that moment, it would have been settled easier. how could I not be the best mom I could be, especially on a zoom call during a mothers quest opportunity."

Julie acknowledged and celebrated me for closing the door. For allowing myself that time and space, for honoring myself and this moment in time. For leading in example of self-care and commitment. This changed my whole everything. It gave me peace and permission and different thoughts that felt so much better.

I was able to feel better about my self-care and my moment.

Being offered a recorded video of this gave me the freedom to just be in the moment. To not feel like I have to take pictures or notes to capture all of the things I know I will want to remember.

Being one on one gave that extra layer of comfort to show up as who I am fully and just be, to allow this moment to be mine.

This opportunity Julie is giving is called: back to
school milestone hike.
but it's not just about school.
it is about ending the chapter before and
beginning anew.
it is about ending well and starting with intention.

During this time, I had tears. I had moments of not
knowing, moments of fluster and Julie was there
to help it all become clear, to help navigate and to
help support.

During my hike I was in so many places: Hawaii
(that I was blessed to experience with my
husband), the nursery I just got home from a bike
ride today, different places my family and I have
hiked (Tahoe, Oakland, pleasant hill, San
Leandro...) but the path was always clear ...hiking
up, being at the top and just acknowledging my
dad, going down the hill-making it to the bottom.

Julie even acknowledged me. And asked me to
basically acknowledge myself.
what did it take to get here?
to invest in yourself.

you did that! you are here. you are investing in yourself. you are doing the work.

how often do you hear that? or think that? or realize that?
how often do we celebrate our actions or acknowledge?

we always end with takeaways and acknowledgements.
I am forever thankful for Julie. she is a gift to this world and she is helping others become their highest selves so that we can all put our gifts in this world.

THIS IS MY YEAR TO SHINE!!!

it has never been clearer, more felt, more real.
so thankful this all happened on thankful Thursday.
what a blessed day

8.20.21
I have always wanted to be a mom
To teach and write books
To own my own home for all of my family

I AM CHOOSING PEACE

Today started rough.
Today a couple of people upset me so much I was
shaking and couldn't shake the feelings.
Today I decided I won't let others decisions affect
my life much.
We will deal with future dates as they come.
We will fight for our hearts, our respect as always.
We will fight for what we feel is right, for what we
know is right, for equality, for fairness, for
happiness.
We will let people do what makes them happy
while not letting it bring us unhappiness.
And we will accept where we stand with people
whether we like it or not.
We will not allow negativity to disturb the peace.
It's ok to feel what's real. To deal and move on.
Thankful for responding vs reacting
Thankful for reacting and being honest
Thankful for understanding
Thankful for choosing peace
3/1/2020

FINALLY HOME

I see you and breathe a breath of fresh air

Literally coronavirus pandemic everywhere.
But coming home to you finally feels like home
It's been so long since I could really feel that in my
bones.
For years I mentally planned how I would escape
my toxic situation
For months I've been running with no luck of
stable placement.
It's hard as a single mother of three
It's depressing feeling like no one got me.
Like no one wants me
Excuse me, I mean we.
You are my new start, what I've been longing for
I took my time avoiding this because I was scared
before.
I am still scared because it is all so much
I still have so much to do in order to level up.
But finally, I know I am home
I can't say it will be forever but for a long while I
know.
Vegas, Patterson, San Leandro, alameda
Ohio, Oakland, Santa Margarita.
Blessed to have family in many places
Blessed to have my kids, the lives I created.
Everyone has found their home and now we are
claiming ours

I know it won't be easy, it's already been so hard.
It can only keep getting better
So thankful to all who've helped because we were
in it together.
Settling down, settling in soon
So excited to lay down roots.
So excited for our life to finally begin
This is it 🖤
3/17/20

PRAYING

Up at 3 in the morning just praying.
 Praying those struggling with addictions find their
way.
Praying my loved ones stay safe during covid 19
and all Illnesses.
Praying for my loved one's mental health during
this time and always.
I know my mom is having a hard time not seeing
us right now.
Praying for those who have lost loved ones.
Praying for those fighting sickness.
Praying for those who are taking care of us.
Praying for the world.
Hoping the Pge bill is affordable with all the extra
electricity we are using being stuck home 24/7.

Up with my diffuser going: on guard and frankincense. Baby rub on. Kids had tea with honey before bed. Oregano +coconut oil on spine and feet. Laundry being done upstairs early because my husband works still and he's been changing clothes/showering to disinfect every day after work. Having to wash clothes after any of us being outside.

I always believe everything should be clean but I also believe we kill our good germs too that help us fight. I believe in outside and happiness is healing and prayer is powerful and too much technology is no good.

Up praying while my family sleeps. Up thankful. Thankful for the weekend, my husband does not have to work. Thankful my cousin is home and safe for her birthday. Thankful my household is healthy. Thankful addiction and temptation and relapse haven't defeated. Thankful for another day.

3/28/20

ENABALING REALITY

I don't like who you become when you drink
How can I not love all of you, as you are - but love you unconditionally?

I will never understand
How you consciously decide to go down that
path.
You are sober when you make the choice to
change it
You are sober when you could decide to not do it.

I know that my thoughts and emotions are mine
I feel like I am allowing your actions to change
mine.
My emotions are spiraling based on the choices
you made
My emotions are tied to you- but that's not fair of
me to put that shame or blame.

I want to be understanding
I don't want to be enabling.

Then I thought of what someone said today,
"Look through the eyes of love".
This morning I left that journaling space blank,
And now I know why that was.

The universe works in mysterious ways
It was written for me before I knew what to say.

When I look through the eyes of love-
I only see you; I only see love.
Your mistakes don't take away the you I fell in
love with
Even if that person disappears for a bit.
When I look through the eyes of love
It's more than enough.

Thankful and grateful and always blessed.
Thankful for poetry.
For my outlet.
For my truth.
For my healing.
Thankful for the opportunity to "begin anew."
As it was said this morning in the mini retreat
"Every breathe is opportunity to start a new."
8/7/20

STILL PROCESSING

Although I have this beautiful book, that I am
proud of.... this month is still a tough month for
me.
Several times I have caught myself in the feelings.

Although I am proud this book will be released on
my dad's 7-year anniversary, his favorite number.
This is a "good" thing....
I still do have some sadness.
It is ok to feel sad. It is ok to not feel sad.

I have been processing so much this month, these
last 7+ years.

*I remember telling you it was ok to go
(When really, I wanted to beg you to stay)
But I wanted you to be at peace
I knew eventually I would be "ok."
so, I told you it was ok to go, as if you needed
permission
as if you needed it to be ok with me
because I knew you were holding on for me.

*I remember saying to you it was ok if you wanted
to go
and immediately thinking "did I just hurt your
feelings? Do you think I want you to go?
Do you think I am tired of fighting this fight with
you? did I just say the wrong thing?"
I questioned if that was the right thing to say

or if I hurt you, as if I wasn't willing to fight
because of your pain.

I remember telling you I would be ok
(I really didn't believe it, but I knew it would be
somewhat true, one day.)
I felt like you needed to hear me say that
So, I said it.

I knew our time was at the end
I didn't want any more suffering.

*Some things no one can understand...
until they can.

and it's not what I would wish for, for anyone
because to understand, you have to lose someone.

and I don't want that for those I love
I don't need you to feel my pain to be there for me
I just need you to be a part of what makes me
happy and helps my healing and peace.
in the beginning that meant going along with my
requests to wear special shirts on special days
wear a button, wear the raiders or A's.

These days it may look like reading "healing while hurting"
these days I don't even know what I need.

I am still a just a girl missing her dad
I am still just a daughter who is processing loss
and it's ok to be sad.
it's ok to let me be not ok
it's ok to not know what to do or say.
sometimes I just need to be with me
sometimes I just need to feel the feelings and
remember the memories.
1/7/21
your anniversary is in 14 days.
I thought a lot before how I would want to see
this day happening.
and the vision was never clear
you never know somethings, until the time is here.

REPITITION

Have you ever lost someone?
Did you find yourself having memories on re-play
in your mind?
Did you notice you had certain things you would
say to yourself that brought you comfort?
Have you ever noticed the repetition?

repetition of feelings, despite the amount of time that has passed.

Repetition of memories shared, because it's all you have left.

Repetition of words, because you run out of words to say-to express yourself.

Have you ever journaled it all and then tried to make it into a book?

How hard it is to pick out the poetry and reflections you will use-when you have years and years of written pages.

How hard it is to leave stuff out when you want to add it all.

How hard it is to find the "right" order of it all.

How hard it is to put yourself out there, knowing you will be judged but knowing this is your calling.

How hard it is to not want anyone to edit something so personal because you want it to be authentic and not be changed by anyone else.

But to know, an editor could have made things "nicer."

Have you ever lost someone, and you still want to make that person proud?

You want to create beauty to maybe help anyone else in similar shoes.

You want to find ways to honor a loved one who
has transitioned.
Have you ever done something with all of your
heart and it not be "good enough" for others?
but it was once good enough for you, even
exceeded that.

You have to remember your why.
Remember your definition of "success"
Embrace the good and also take the "bad" as good
too and let it all feel however is present but do not
live there, with any of it.
Because you still have more work to do.
And you still have so much to always be proud of.

so be proud. be excited.
you can always make changes.
you can always edit.
but make sure you are doing it for you.
I hope you keep your happiness and I hope you
keep on shining.

This is just the beginning.
It always is.
1/1/21

YOU

Today I thought about you, as a YOU.
I wondered what your journey will be.
Because although I wrote you, I am not you and
you are not me.
 Although we are.
We are also, not.
I truly believe you will have your own journey,
purpose and lessons.

I think that's the beautiful thing about books.
Books are magical.
They take on impacts of their own.
I can't know what to expect.

I have so much more in me to write and release.
So much more I want to do and create.
So much more.

For me, I love books in physical form.
I love holding them, owning them, sharing them.

Today I got a notice in email saying your order has
been shipped from our facility-
I had ordered in the 10th

This particular order is to Lindsey to be in the tiny
book photoshoot.
I am thankful for that.

But now I realize I haven't received an email like
this for the 7 prints I ordered for myself. I had
ordered on the 8th
And I'm still waiting

I am more anxious, constantly learning steps.

Do I order even more, since it all takes time?
Ordering, waiting for shipping, waiting to receive,
any mail delays, holidays and what not.

I think the beauty of this is not knowing
(sometimes)
There's so much pressure in every piece of this.
It's nice when there's not.

Today I thought of you, As you.
A book.
My book.
But you, as your own.

I wonder in what hands you will land

And what you will bring to all who get a chance to experience you.
I wonder what your purpose will be.
I wonder what you have in store for me.
What do you have in store...?

Excited to find out
Also, nervous
But mostly, inspired and empowered.

Thank you for choosing me.
12/19/20

I WONDER

I wonder what day my books will show up in the mail
will I open it to find mistakes like the ones many have posted?
will the cover look, ok?
I get emotional just thinking of what the moment could feel like
I can't wait to read this book; I too want to read it...I have not read it.
I know I wrote it,
But I have not read it.
I wonder what that will feel like...

It isn't the exact vision I had planned; it took
several changes.
I wonder who will want to purchase those first 6,
the ones I will sign...
should I have ordered more?
the wait will be even longer to order more.
I know I want it, as is.
I do not plan on making changes.
I hope any errors, aren't too big.
I am looking forward to the day-that mail comes.
I don't know when to expect it.
I don't even know what to expect.
I wonder how it will feel to hold my very own
book...
Will it feel completely real?

I already want to write and publish more.
I'm already scared again.
already questioning if it's possible.
already held back by fears.

I wonder how much more this accomplished book
has in store...
I wonder what will come from it...
I already want to put out different "upgraded"
versions.

I can't wait to see the books get here...
to find their way home.
I hope I am happy with the outcome
I hope it feels like success, I hope it feels "good
enough."

I hope it makes you proud dad
and I hope the memories live on through
strangers, loved ones and your spirit-through this
book
12/16/20

DIG DEEPER

There's so much I didn't know.
There's so much I never asked. Never thought to
ask.
Questions I now have.
There are things I did know and I didn't ask you to
dig deeper.
I didn't ask for more.
Now I want more
And you are not here to provide words.
You shared some pains with me and I don't know
why we didn't conversation about it all.

You shared some truths of your hurt and I didn't always understand how you could forgive after it all.
7 years you've been gone.
And I'm barley just starting to do what I should have done....
Dig deeper
Ask questions
Show interest
And learn more.

I'm sorry it took so long
Trying to get to know you while your gone is tough.
Wanting to know the parts of you that I didn't.
Wanting to know your history, because that's my history.
Learning about you, teaches me about me.
I need to know my family.

Connections is how you will stay alive.
You through me, you through them— this is how you survive.
Stories, memories, history

Thank you for continuing to help me on this
healing journey
Love you dad
2.26.21

NOT READY FOR YOU TO BE JUST A MEMORY

I've been through it before
Didn't feel fair to have to once more.
It's like I knew what to expect,
But still hoped for the best.
Did some things different, learned from the past
Did some things the same, even knowing better
than that.
No one's day is guaranteed
But yet when doctors diagnose us with an end
date, we start to think and act differently.
I'm not ready for you to be just a memory
I'm not ready for the pain of losing another who
means so much to me.
I'm not ready for my kids to experience loss again
I'm not ready for the journey of a wound that can't
heal but I'm grieving and healing, even before
death happens.
I'm not ready for regrets or wishes that will never
come true
I'm not ready for death, I'm not ready to lose you.

And yes, I know the truth
I know this battle has been hard on you.
.....
I know you deserve to be pain free
You deserve a cure that could never be.
I deserve life with you here
You deserve life with me here.
All we have is right now
And that has to be enough somehow.
2/12/21

DETOX

Why do I want to want you?
I've gone so long without you.
I've proven to myself I can live without you,
But living without "having" you doesn't mean I
haven't thought about you.
I thought I missed you,
I'm pretty sure I do.
I know you are "no good" for me,
I know there's "better" alternatives for me.
But even after so long of not being involved,
I made the choice to welcome you in like it would
mean "problem solved."

But missing you was never the problem,

Freedom of choice, or lack of- was never the
problem.
I am growing and changing,
But part of me was still holding on to the past and
what used to "work for me."
Not all of me is fully embracing,
And that is now why I'm up at 2 in the morning,
since 1 in the morning.

Mentally, physically-feeling the downside effects
of choices made,
Missing you and allowing you back in has me in
discomfort, maybe some pain.

It's so crazy what a detox will show you...
It's so real what temptation will show you...
How it will all grow you,
The truth it will hold for you.

Sometimes we go back,
Thinking we want that.
Sometimes we think the life we knew is easier to
live,
Sometimes we forget what living is.
But we are just forever learning,
Experimenting to create a life worth living.

On a quest to create better health,
To find the highest version of self.
And I'm learning sleep is a big part of that,
And learning what is interrupting that.

I wasn't making completely healthy choices by not
choosing you,
But now I am reminded just how much healthier
those choices were because of the feeling I now
have from having you.

I could keep going down this route and I'm sure
eventually I can adapt,
Or I can choose a new path, I don't have to go
back.

This idea of the satisfaction you used to bring,
Keeps the idea of you tempting.
But truth is, I didn't actually like how you made me
feel,
It's all a mental game that leads a real negative
physical feel.

Addiction is a real struggle,
Conditioning is a real cycle.

I thought I deserved you, like you were a prize.
But the real prize was here, without you this
whole time🖤✨🙏

(Sometimes poetry comes to by 3am because you
are up reflecting for hours unable to sleep)
Breaking free is the lifestyle
4.5.21

MY ZEN

I am trying to find my zen
I have been practicing yoga almost daily, over a
month in.
I am in a live class, in hopes to be more intentional
I am working on being on camera, in hopes to be
present and mindful.
I invested money because I know it's worth it
I set alarms because I know I don't want to miss it.
It is so easy to get distracted by my "to do" list
It is so easy to get frustrated, with my
environment.
I am working on creating the space that will best
serve me
I am working on making changes so that I can
show up as the best me.
I am working on getting sleep

waking up, drinking water, having a morning
routine.
I am working on progress and not perfection
Every day I am grateful, trying to soak in every
little win.
I am working on my zen
Wanting to yell less, when I am frustrated.
Wanting to control my emotions with more
intention
wanting to respond and not just give reactions.
Down here on my mat, I see from a different view
I begin to want to sweep, mop and even vacuum.
Down here from this view I see things I want to
re-arrange
like shoes and underneath the bed, that has
become a storage space.
While on screen I see me
and I don't always like what I see.
I can get distracted by seeing me
I get distracted with my backgrounds, in my own
screen.
I start to see things I want to change
I go on and off screen as I try to decide if showing
up with all this reality is ok.
It is so much easier to turn the camera off

to see one good picture of myself, that feels good
enough.
It is so much more calming to turn my camera off
to know I won't be as distracted with all of my
"turn offs".
but with my camera off, it's also easier to be less
accountable
I want to challenge myself; I want to be teachable.
I want to build community
and to me, it starts with me.
It starts by showing up
By being vulnerable, honest and open to change
the "hard" stuff.

I am thankful for how far I have come
I am thankful for my growth and how far I still
want to go
I feel like there is no end to this learning road
there will always be a new goal.
there will always be something to work on
I will never be complete as is but I will feel better
as time goes on.
4/4/21

FRIDAY FEELS

Today I faced new challenges, as my legs are very
sore from 16minutes of 21-day fix beachbod
yesterday
I did not dress in my yoga attire and that did also
not serve me as well
kids came in with their emotions at one point and I
got upset, I found my way back to re-ground-,
there will be time after to get to this moment of
what doesn't need to be present

I am enjoying my socks off, my feet on the ground.
I am enjoying feeling all I physically feel -that tells
me I really did put in work yesterday physically.
I am thankful to be cleaning house and getting it
ready for the day, even if it gets dirty as I am
cleaning. I know that I am getting things done.
Day two of national poetry month.
Yesterday I did not write a poem but I did walk
and mail 3 of our poetry books to people. I did
share about our book.
I plan to make a step each day when it comes to
poetry, one of my all-time loves.

Friday is here with all the Feels
4/4/21

September 6, 2020 ·

It's not your time
You've faced this crossroads now a couple of times.
Last time you made it out
I knew this day would come but we are never expecting it "now."
You were supposed to keep getting better
Why is this happening? I hear it never really gets better.
The feeling I'm feeling is so heavy
I need to remember to breathe.
Sounds easy, but it's not
These emotions are too much, pass me some ....
I know, smoking is just a mask
To fix what can't be fixed- it can't.
Do I have a beer for you?
If I cry too much, will you hear and pull through?
If I cry too much does that mean you can't go peacefully?
Please tell me what you need from me.
But you can't, I can't hear you
I've reached that moment that I'd do anything to hear you.
Reaching out to people who are spiritual healers

Reaching out to hear, to feel, to get some
answers.
I believe everything happens for a reason
But right now, I can't make any sense of this
lesson.
I know death is just a part of life
I know it's ok to not be ok and right now I just
don't feel right.

I'm angry, I'm sad, I'm confused, I have regrets
I'm hopeful, I'm strong, I'm weak and upset.

Do I explain it to the youngest grandkids or do I
wait?
They feel it, they are the purest to reach you at
this stage.
We will all support each other
This journey is forever.
This healing is lifelong
This hard part feels so rushed and yet so long.

(My prayers to my loved ones. My heart hurts
with you and for you. I know this feeling all too
well. Writing this from a stage of my phase while
feeling your emotions all too real. Feels like just
yesterday for me and it's been years. Dad, please

help us all from heaven. To my cousin Sonya thank you for your gifts.
 All of us down here- we will be in this life together) I swear my purpose for meeting and becoming family becomes clearer. I swear my journey was for a bigger reason beyond me.

I'm seeing it all, now more than ever. Now in new ways.
I've always known but now is a new page.

Please send prayers in the universe and to my loved ones.
Having to let a loved one go is the hardest ever.
Especially a parent. A son. A brother. An uncle. A grandpa.

Explore more
Try again ... even if you've done it before...
Take your time, explore more.
Take charge and be a Tour guide
Trust in the present, plan for next time.
Trust that it was meant for you
Scarcity mindset will have you fooled.
Tuesday's travels have ended safely
Time to get back to "reality."

6/15/21

Trust in flow
fine.... I will trust in the flow
I will walk into the unknown.
That money saved, that I say "I do not have"
I'll use that.
I'll finally go buy those plants
my heart has been yearning for that.
I'll take that trip to do what needs to be done
because bills do have to be taken care of.

Faith, GOD, prayer- the universe provides
I hear people say it all the time.
I have experienced magic and miracles before
I know I can experience it some more.
where and when did scarcity mindset take over
who I am?
I know abundance goes beyond me; I am grateful-I
am.

Fine, I believe.

But you can't just say it and not mean it
you have to really believe it.
or else the results won't be what you hope for

you have to go deeper.
you have to really walk in faith
that's what it takes.
manifestation takes more than just hope
manifestation takes feeling it in your soul.

fine, I'll give it a try
I'll take action and walk on the wild side.
I'll take leaps of faith and step into my power
step into my purpose and bloom like a flower.
because I am already living proof
that circumstance only holds you back, when you
allow it to.

fine....
I can be so much more than "fine"
day 3 #diveintopoetry
7/8/21

SOUL-STICE

*I keep reading solstice but I keep hearing soul-
stice
something about daily practices,
practice of abundance, it's all around
my children helped plant seeds and now a garden
can be found,

385

we have bees in our yard thanks to my brave
cousin
we have grown to share space with them,
I can't say we love them but we don't fear them as
we once did
we keep water in a plate for them and plants near
to help them live.
we have an apple tree and we love to share with
any who ask
the neighbors have a plum tree, but the
relationship for asking isn't one where we'd be
likely to get a yes,
so, we pick the ones that lean over our fence
plums are my favorite.
We have beautiful flowers growing, and we also
have food coming to form
we are surprised by bugs, butterflies-even
hummingbirds.
something about this garden is so good for my
soul
it feeds us, it provides beauty and teaches us
lessons we didn't know.
this garden provides the children ways to make
money by helping care for it
some plants will survive mistakes and neglect and
some only are here for certain seasons.

I love being on the hammock, on a warm day
smelling the fresh air after rain,
putting my bare feet on the ground
listening to the birds and our children make their
sounds.
soul-stice.
#diveintopoetry

July 2, 2021. EARTHLY HEAVENLY BIRTHDAY
Both are true, I am happy and sad,
Both are true, I am grieving and healing from
"losing" my dad.
Life is what happens, so I tried not to make any
plans,
Life is what happens, So I tried to just allow it to
happen.
Happy heavenly birthday dad
day 1 #diveintopoetry
7/7/21

WISHES FOR MANIFESTING

wish...I have wished, hoped and prayed for many
things
I am starting to see prayers have been answered,
even if not in the exact way I wish for the answers
to be seen.

wishes on candles for birthdays, wishes on
dandelions
wishes when the clock turns 11:11, wishes in
prayer filled moments.

where do these practices come from? when did I
learn to believe?
what really is a wish? is it what happens with
manifesting?
does wishing mean you believe in GOD, in magic,
in the universe?
does wishing mean you are hopeful; does it mean
you can also get hurt?
hurt from getting your hopes up and not receiving
what you want so badly
hurt from answered prayers, but not the answers
you wanted so desperately.

do wishes hold power? do they hold truth?
do wishes really ever come true?

do your wishes define you?
are you ready for what you actually said you
wanted? what if it was given to you?

I am starting to look at my reality differently

I have gotten many things I have wished for, but I didn't notice quickly.
I noticed through complaining...because I wasn't happy, it didn't look or feel like -exactly what I wanted
complaining helped me become grateful and change my perspective, it was most honest.
I had to feel the real feelings before I could make that shift
that shift to realization, that I am living that wish....

I have gotten what I asked for, many times
now I wonder how many times was I too blind to realize?

and although answers come in many forms and signs
we are always in control, of what it could all look and feel like.
we can always change, we can always re-write
we are life-long learners, just trying to live life.
#diveintopoetry day 4
7/9/21

July 24, 2020 ·
I just don't know why you didn't say no

So many reasons I'm sure, so many - I know.
I just don't know why you didn't say no
You were sober, you had control.
You didn't want it enough, the life without it.
You wanted it too much, the life with it.
I wish you would've said no
You knew you'd be asked but you said you'd say
no.
I am so thankful you made it home
You will never be alone.
These choices tear us apart
It's not that it makes loving you hard.
But it does hurt
I keep praying for the tools that will work.
I am learning how to take control of my reactions
and thoughts
I am allowing myself to feel, I'm not saying I'm not.
But I'm choosing to no longer repeat
It's a thin line between recovery and defeat.
We are indeed a team
But we also have our own journey, our individual
story.
I love who you are when you are your best self
I know you can be even more but you have to
want it for yourself.
I am thankful for your life

I am thankful to be by your side.
Even in the hard times
I am learning every time.

You get another chance to say no
And I'm just thankful
Fun filled Friday,

Freedom to choose,
Fears are real,
Feel the feels,
Fill up your tank,
Finish that task,
Fight or flight,
Fix what you can,
Faith over fear,
Flowing not forcing

UNREAL, UNHEALED

it doesn't seem real
that time can pass and wounds still feel unhealed.
that so much time can pass without you here,
that the mind knows you are gone but still tries to
talk the brain into thinking you are near.
it doesn't seem real, death
it's very real, I know it is, life is very different.

391

and living isn't the same as it was living in a world
with you
living isn't living when I spend so much time
missing you.
I spend so much time wanting you back
but not wanting you in the pain cancer gave you,
no one wants to re-live that.
I find peace knowing you are at peace now
but I am selfish wishing it was all different
somehow.
I lost an uncle, a role model for all boys and men
but my heart aches for my cousins who lost a
father and my aunt who lost her husband.

how was this post from 3 years ago, me hearing
the news?
how has it been 3 years that life has been going
on without you?
it's crazy how the soul knows things before we
realize
just yesterday I ordered a picture of you for our
fridge and today saw the date .... Of when you
"died."
you aren't dead, you just aren't here
that was no coincidence, that was you, your soul
was here.

thank you for visiting me
thank you for the memories.

sending love to my cousins and aunt, especially
today.
7/24/20

Lena Velasquez
July 27 at 3:03 PM ·
7/26/21
#9 but it's 10...
#diveintopoetry

I am living in someone's past
it's night time here but morning there...who is the
future? who is the present?

time on the clock will fool you if you let it
not enough time, will consume you- if you fall for
it.

I am working on living, now
intentionally creating my past, right now.
intentionally creating my future, in this moment
it all exists- here, in the present.

the only illusion are the ones from doubt and fear
trust in the unknown, "faith over fear."

BEGIN AGAIN
let me begin again
I shouldn't have yelled because of my frustration.
you are only responding based on what you have
learned
what you are feeling and not always having the
words.

let me begin again
I need to step back and breathe in.
I need to reflect on better ways
I am, doing the same as you when I behave this
way.
Triggered by so much
when did I lose touch?
when did it become too much?
when did I abuse my touch?

it is not ok
not ok to respond this way.
because I know it is ok to not be ok
and yet I am not allowing you to cope this way.

394

let me begin again
I am sorry I lost my patience.
I am sorry I was caught in a moment
I am trying to own it.
I am a parent but sometimes I make mistakes
Sometimes I need a break.
Sometimes we cause pain when we don't take
care of ourselves
sometimes yelling hurts more than someone else.

let me begin again
I would like to handle this different.
7/23/21
#diveintopoetry day 8

LAST YEAR (IN 2020)

I remember being in last year and feeling finally
free
free from what all of the "shoulds" used to tell me
I had to be.
Free from the fear of the world as it was crashing
free from the depression that used to feel
suffocating.

I was just coming into new thoughts when the
pandemic was "just starting"

I was believing in being outside, exercising, fresh
air and flowing.
I was just now learning to not be consumed by
social media, the news and fear
I was just now growing into a different me, last
year.

The dreams of finding the right space to teach at
were put on hold again
I was led to dive into lifelong dreams of becoming
an author for the first time, during a pandemic.
I came into money I couldn't have expected to
receive
I started to invest that money differently.
I invested in groups, in people I believed in
I invested in coaching, in self-care but this time
self-care looked different.
It wasn't about manicures and pedicures and new
clothes or shoes
It was about furniture we always wanted,
chiropractic care and date times too.

I said yes more intentionally, as well as "no"
I started making connections and watched myself
grow.
I started to learn to love me even more

I started to tell myself "Let's not go back to
scarcity anymore"
Let's not go back to putting me last
I'm a better me by making me a priority and I can't
go back.

I remember ending last year, worried how the next
could compare
knowing it didn't have to, but feeling kind of
scared.
Knowing what to kind of expect from the
pandemic now
knowing we could never know what to expect
anyhow.

I remember saying "let's not go back"
let's not come back to the kind of fear that keeps
me stuck in my tracks.
let's not come back to the situations that bring my
anxiety so high, that the low parts are so low and
too hard to get up

let's not come back to the places that no longer fill
us up.
I wanted to keep the faith, the prosperity and the
growth

I wanted to keep the tools I have gained to
support my roads.

We are more than halfway in this new year now
That scarcity has shown up several times, that fear
has come around.
my anxiety has risen on several occasions
my depression has tried to come stay for a while,
during certain moments.
reality will always be whatever it is
the truth will always be true, that's just realistic.

I also know that reality can be what we make it to
be
it may never be "perfect" but the truth is, it can
be...
it can be imperfectly perfect
I am learning to live in the moments.
moment by moment, going with the flow
it doesn't mean no work is involved.

it takes so much to create change in our own
behaviors
to create habits, that aren't too familiar.
to do inner healing work and release the past

to give ourselves grace through the mistakes we
will make-that sometimes pull us back.
it's not easy to feel our emotions and create new
thoughts
to take new action steps and truly go after what
we want.

It's not easy to not go back
back to what we worked so hard to get away from
but yet it's still somehow attached.
attached to pieces of who we once were
attached to pieces of us that still feel so familiar.
it's not easy to not fall back into those old stories
we used to tell
the stories that sometimes still feel real.

because they are still real, except now I have new
mindset
I have reframed those stories to tell something
different
stories of transformation, growth and change
stories of healing, even while some pain still
remains.
My perspectives have shifted
I have elevated.

sometimes, I am still that me
But I am also this me...

what if, it's not about not going back
what if, it's about walking hand in hand....

that going back and what's here now
can all live together somehow.

that it doesn't have to be "one or the other"
it doesn't have to mean "better or worse."
all it means is embracing each other
all it means is continuing to do the work.

because this work is never ending
it's constant growing, constant new beginnings.
It's constant learning
And constant healing.
I am constantly becoming
maybe I will go back...maybe it doesn't have to be
a bad thing.
maybe acceptance and this new realization will
change it all
I definitely feel more peaceful to move forward, I
just had to talk myself through it all.
Day 6 #diveintopoetry

400

7/14/21

CAN'T BE DIMMED

Due to divine reasons, my light can't be dimmed
Even when I show up during my lowest points, I
still show up as is.
And somehow, as is- is always more than enough
I never leave a space untouched.
When I speak, I speak with honesty
When I take action, I do with integrity.

I know that if I were to die tonight
I will still impact lives.
Due to divine reasons, my light can't be dimmed
For even when my body is no more- my soul will
live on in spirit.
I will leave so much of me behind
Time goes on, and I'll be with time.

Due to divine reasons, my light can't be dimmed
Because I am learning to live in my purpose, I am
flowing from within.
When you allow yourself to align with your
callings
No one can answer that call but you- only you
have your specific heart beating.

Even in a pause, your pulse can be felt
Even in life after, there's some of you in someone
else.

When I show up as me
I am always surprised by reality.
Somehow messages come to me
Somehow messages come from me.
Due to divine reasons, my light can't be dimmed
I don't even know all that's in store, I just know I
feel this.

#diveintopoetry day 7....
written Friday 7/16/21
I came across this quote" due to divine reasons,
my light can't be dimmed"
I don't know who made that quote, I couldn't find
the person. But it spoke to me and the rest flowed
to me.

FIND YOUR FUEL

Instructions on how to live are all around us
everything is teaching us different and similar
stuff.
you find answers within the living

you will come to your own instructions based on
what you start experiencing.
tell about it all, share your stories
tell your truths, tell your fears, tell it all -honestly.
your words matter and may become teaching
points for someone else
your life matters and may become inspiration for
even yourself.
pay attention and ask the questions
pay attention to what you wouldn't normally pay
attention to, ask what everyone else isn't asking
gratitude always helps me.
it helps me know life is always great and helps me
see through the struggle differently.

lately my eyes have been tired of the screens
lately I don't want the iPhone that hears
everything I'm saying even when I'm not using it
but yet it somehow hears me.
lately I found rest a priority
lately I found that sleep is such an important part
of living.
you have to re-find and re-define what you want
spending your time to look like
you have to dream again and trust in what reality
can be like.

it doesn't have to be multi-tasking all the time
it doesn't have to be putting yourself at the end of
the line.
fear loves making you sick
fear loves holding you hostage.
fear loves keeping you safe
fear loves thriving on your name.

you get to re-build, anytime- however many times
you get to continuously heal- anytime- however
many times.
you get to find what fuels you
you get to create your instruction manual- if you
want to.
Day 12 #diveintopoetry
7/28/21

CHURCH

Take me to church, it's been so long since I've
been
I have no excuses, not even the pandemic we are
still in.
I have made time for other trips, people and
places
I have made exceptions, choices and
commitments.

404

I miss church, for what it was
I know whatever it is like now, is still more than
enough.
It can't become any greater or less than
you go for the word of GOD, that is always
relevant.
It's all about your belief system
It's all about your spiritual senses.
It's all about the messages you receive
it's all about what you make it mean.
...and yet I have not been to church since pre-
pandemic
I tried joining virtually and was never as
interested.

before the pandemic shut everything down
I was really lost while being found.
I used to feel so horribly when missing Sunday
service
I used to connect "missing church" with
consequences.
It wasn't a healthy way to live
during this pandemic I had to change the way I
lived and viewed this.
I found church within me
I found spaces and places with people virtually.

I found soul care and the courageous life society
I found time at home and making time for me a
priority.
I found church at home, in the hardest of times
lighting candles and saying prayers-are always
available anytime.

I have come "home" even more, now
I am not saying I do not need or long for attending
church now.
recently, Sunday morning soccer has become our
place to be
our family right now has different priorities.
now that life is getting back to "normal"
we have to continue to decided what do we want
to be "our normal."
I do believe I want Sunday service back in my life
I guess the real way to know is to go and see what
it feels like.
I know I miss it
I know I view life somewhat differently that I once
did.

I know church is a part of me
whether or not apart from me.

but I'm ready to go back, in person
I'm so ready to sit in Sunday service....
day 5 #diveintopoetry
7/12/21

LEVELS OF LISTENING

I am always listening for it
for the lessons, for the messages, for-all of "it."
The stuff that isn't said
the stuff we don't want to hear and would rather
hear instead.
I am always listening for it
because I care about it.
I enjoy going "deeper"
I enjoy authenticity and being sincere.

The world doesn't get to tell you: how, when, why,
who
only you do, if- you choose to.
The world will try to tell you anything you allow it
to
do you want their truth? or can you find it for
you?

I am always listening
yes, especially when I am "just" observing.

7/26/21

UNFOLDING

I am constantly coming out on the other side
I chose my battles last night.
I went in with no intentions to fight
I had made up my mind.
your words of hurt no longer boil me over
revisiting the past doesn't make it alive for me
anymore.
I can re-visit without going back
I no longer live in the past.

I can put myself in your shoes
but I refuse to feel guilty for not sharing the same
truth.

***I am allowing ease in with flow
I am allowing trust in the unknown.
I am feeling all of the feelings
I am choosing to respond over reacting.
I am bringing in the ease when it comes to my
intentions
honesty allows for me to have peace within.
I am allowing me to be me
no agenda, no force- just imperfect and free.

I am allowing my story to be told
...and let the rest unfold.
8/2/21

GRASPING

I put it all out there, what came up
Still left some things out, I remember now that it's
"done."
Came to a compromise, that wasn't really a
compromise
It was a settlement, again for your benefit and I
didn't want to fight.
So, I allowed it to be enough
But we all know, again the same stuff will come
up.
This "compromise" is just to stall time
The only difference is, I'm starting to realize.
I'm not impatient, I'm just becoming done with the
cycles
Kind of over the patterns and understanding my
rights too.
I'm starting to grasp my real power
And you're starting to grasp that loss of power.
And I know it hurts you
That's not what I want it to do.

But at some point, something has to change in
order to get change
So much is at stake and deserves a chance at
change.
....
So, I'll keep moving forward, one step at a time
Because it's all been long overdue and my heart
deserves some peace of mind.
8/2/21

COURAGEOUS CONVERSATIONS

How do you prepare for courageous
conversations?
When you've been holding the contemplation, on
your heart for so many years
When your traumatized by past attempts
And you're tired of fighting the internal tears.

You just want change
And change begins with the courage to say...
To say what's been on your heart, yes again
Courage to attempt a different outcome, even if in
the past it didn't.

Knowing that no matter how it all goes

It has to be for the best right? Because it's a step
forward -even in the unknown.
Scared because we think we know what to expect
Scared because from what we know, change in
the way we wish isn't what's to be expected.

But still hopeful for what could possibly be
Still can't give up on me.
I have to speak
I'm ready.

I'm ready for the war, if that what it takes
But I'm hoping for understanding and ability in my
decisions to make.
Praying you allow me to be heard
Praying you really hear me and stop fighting my
words.
I don't need you to agree or give in
I just want you to actually listen.
Listen enough to compromise
Listen enough to have my best interest in mind.

Listen to respond and not react
Talk with me and not at me, be on my team
instead of against.

I know you too will have your own feelings to
process based on what I will share
I know you care
But I need you to allow me to be human too
I need you to allow my truth too.
8/1/21

UNFINISHED

Don't let me go
Part of me is so tired and feels like it's ok to go.
But the other part of me screams no
No, not yet
Tears fall from exhaustion.
No, not yet
So much is unfinished.
I still have dreams
Don't take me.
... I want to say to you, don't let me go
I feel like I'm fading away and I'm wondering if you
even know.
7/30/21

SAY IT FROM LOVE
In this moment, I don't know what to do
All I can do is hurt with you.
All I can do is listen to you

I know loss, I have no words for you.
I won't tell you it gets better
Because for me, this pain is forever.
Because for me, thoughts still creep in and I beat
myself up about what I could have done better
I still have moments of flooded tears that feel like
they will go on forever.

I have been avoiding this moment for a long time
now
I've been keeping my words to hello and goodbye,
sometimes when I pass by, I just look down.
Because I have so much from love to say
But I just don't know what to say.
So, I stay silent
I avoided this moment.

But today, today I stepped into it
Asked you how you are doing, although not ready
for the answer to it.
I realize all I can do is acknowledge your story
All I can do is share some of my journey.

I'm so thankful you took some time to talk
Sometimes that is support enough.
Sometimes taking the time

May have saved someone's life.

Looking at you walk away
I see how much of you has physically changed.
How much weight you've lost...?
The way you carry yourself has changed a lot.

You walked away and some of your pain stayed
with me
You walked away and left some of your story.

"Enjoy them, every moment. Now is the time to
spend time with your children. "
I can't say I know what it's like to lose a child just
the thought is too hard to think of.
I have met loss; I have met grief- and it's a tough
part of life to come to terms with. To learn to
accept and find growth with. I'm not sure we find
closure; I don't think that's what we truly look for.
We just continue to find ways to deal. We just
continue to learn what helps us heal. And maybe
we turn it into more, by sharing words with each
other. Support can look like so many things.
8/13/21

ONGOING HEALING

I just don't know what to say
I guess that's why sometimes I look the other way.
I guess that's why sometimes I go the other way
I guess that's why sometimes I am silent when
there's so much, I can say.

I just don't know the "right" thing to say
Besides it's ok...
It's ok to not be ok...
It's ok to feel what you feel and say what you
have to say.

It's ok for me to just listen
It's ok for me to say "from my experience."
It's ok for me to say "I don't know"
Because truth is, I don't.

I can relate, and yet I can't
7 years later, sometimes I still don't understand.
I remember the nights of sleep that didn't feel like
sleep
Because it was nightmares instead of restful
dreams.
I remember the nights and days of mostly being
awake

Of not wanting to be home because being home
was filled with everything I didn't want to face.

I hear you. I do.
I see you. I do.
I feel your words of truth
I'm sorry this part of life has happened to you.

Loss is never easy
It's a forever type of hurting.
This healing is ongoing
Sometimes you go backwards after so much
growing.
But it isn't growth vs lack
It's just life ...and death is a part of that.
8/12/21

COMMITTED EXHAUSTION

all of these commitments I have been committed
to.
all of these steps towards finish lines, goals and
dreams...
somewhere in there, I still lost me.
in all the self-care and goodness of so much
somewhere in there, I failed to realize when it was
all too much.

I have been feeling very drained lately
sometimes I know what it means.
sometimes it means, not so much yoga or less
screens
sometimes it means more sleep and better
eating/drinking.
sometimes it means just get outside
sometimes it means rest, naps, journal time.

as groups and memberships are coming to "re-
commitment"
as people are asking me to join new opportunities
and activities
I now have to take my time with saying yes
I need to take my time with saying no
I need to spend some time to really feel into it all,
not so much think
because as of now-It's all in my reach.
But just because you can say yes-doesn't mean
you should
just because it's worked for you in the past-
doesn't mean timing is still good.

I feel like I just need a break from it all
I don't want to wonder what whomever will think
of me

I don't want the stress of thinking about the loss it
would mean to say no or take a break
I don't want the guilt that isn't mine
I don't want to drain life, drain time.

I think I just need a pause on it all, a rest on
everything,
not a re-start but a recharge
I want to enjoy the good
I want to feel good

I have things that need my focus
I don't want to lose me in any process.

I am starting to realize just how much I have had
on my plate
how much I "ate."
Realizing, how much is still there
and really taking a moment to ask my body mind
and soul what feels nourishing.
because right now I just feel drained
and I wonder how is that possible, with all the
greatness I have been jumping into,
with all the goodness surrounding me,
with all of the amazing people on my "team,"
how is it I feel so drained?

well.... growth takes change and I have been doing
a lot of healing and learning and finding my way.

it's not easy
even when it's been easy.
I didn't realize just how much work it's been
until I started noticing just how much I have been
feeling and how much I've been doin...

it's ok to pause
it's ok to take a break
it's ok to say no or not right now
it's ok to change
8/19/21

TRAUMATIZED STILL

Although it wasn't a "successful" steal
I have been traumatized still.
I have had nightmares ever since
The kids have had concerns and questions.
It was an attempted theft
Car damages have been "fixed."
The mental damage however, is taking time
No matter how positively I talk to my mind.
I feel like I have to be on alert
Even with all of my gratitude, this hurts.

Even with solutions...
I'm still human.
And I've been impacted by what took place
I'm working through it... I guess this is what it
takes.
8/18/21

Can't be real
This can't be real, it can't be
that Heaven is trying to take you away from me.
I see you laying in that hospital bed
they say it's time to say goodbye but I say I saw
you move your head.
I saw you try to open your eyes; they say that's
not what I saw
I saw you move to our voices; they say that's not
what happened at all.
we have been here before, not that long ago
the doctors said we needed to say goodbye and
we chose not to let go.
you made it out after many days, we all said "we
knew doctors were wrong"
you would never be the same but you will always
be you to us.
you are a fighter and I know you are fighting

I have seen you win before-even when they said
you were dying.
I feel like they want us to make this decision so
fast
this decision to pull the plug as if it's that easy to
grasp.
how can they ask that so easy?
do they not care what you mean to me?
do they just want to make space?
do they just not care because you aren't special to
them, to them you are just another name.
another face they will replace
but for us you are more than words can say.
I know you have already been through a lot
I am sorry if we are putting you through too much.
I am sorry if we are holding on, if you have given
up
I wish I knew what to do, I wish this wasn't so
tough.
covid adds an extra layer of anger, pain and
confusion
we all can't go in and be by your side during a time
when we need to have inclusion.
how can they ask us to say goodbye?
but not allow us to be by your side.
how can they ask us to let you go?

but not let us all in to really know.
I should be with you every step of the way
to make sure they are doing everything because
you deserve to be saved.
I wish you could let me know if I'm standing in the
way
I know GODS got you, you've been saved.
I just can't accept this reality
this reality of you not being here with me,
possibly.
I know I can't expect you to survive every time
I know I can't believe the doctors are telling lies.
but I just can't not see you making it through
and I just can't trust what they are saying about
you.
I know you too well, you are so strong
I love you too much, I can't be as strong.
trying to make sense of all that happening
and I just can't figure out why this is happening.
I love you dad
(My dad passed away years ago.... I didn't write
this for me. But for people I love. And I can relate
to some)
8/29/20

Mystics society posted: where did I come from?

And so much wanted to flow out from me, thanks
to that question
Where did I come from? Woah!
I come from the connection of Chantal Madeleine
Giordano and Juan Ramon Ayala. I come from
their parents whose names I do and don't know. I
come from childhood financial struggles of food
stamps, lots of moving and switching schools. I
come from poetry and pen to paper. I come from
people and experiences that showed me what I
didn't want to be like, but with gratitude enough
to hold for every person and experience has their
value and journey that I may not ever know. I
come from lessons learned and mistakes still to be
made. I come from dreams and inner callings. I
come from, my parents' choice to keep me. I come
from a higher powers saving grace. I come from
what's destined and unknown all at the same
time......
I come from the choices
The "yes's"
The "no's"
The conditioning and upbringing
And finding myself, outside of the rules and
"shoulds"

I come from a family filled with so many different
experiences and pathways that helped mold me
I come from growth and being open to be born
again, as many times as I feel the need to
I come from life
And I came to live
9/1/21

Still, our real
I have been with you for more than half of my life
I have put you first 99% of that time.
We are 16 years into this
I am 31 and still going through our age 17
situations.
I would say age 15, but back then I didn't really
know
Now I know, and still, I don't.
You are a great human being
When you are sober, you are perfection to me.
Obviously, I know- you are not perfect
And, you are dealing with a lot of things I can't fix.
Parts of you, you can't heal
It's been so long, how is this still our real?
2/7/21

DECIDE

I can't keep calling
I can't keep threatening
I have stopped reacting
I started responding.
When you choose to drink or do drugs (alcohol is
a drug)
It continues to take from me and us.
I will forever love you
But I have to love me too.
I have to decide what loving me looks like
I have to take some kind of control, over my life.
Our kids deserve for us to be our best self's
They are getting older and crying out for help.
I need you to do better, longer
I need forever.
2/7/21

LIFE IS SHORT, GIVE ME MORE

We are a week away from valentine's day
I keep feeling you stray away.
Porn in your search history
Girls in your search history.
Years ago, it would've hit me differently
I am broken, I am not me.

I lost you years ago
You cheated, and it's taken its toll.
Our whole first 8 years was you cheating
The last 8 years has been us, re-building.
But the battle of addiction has always been
And with that comes so much other interference.
I want so much more for us
It's 11 pm and I feel done.
What you are doing is not ok
There's not much left for me to say.
There's no point in me being angry
I am disappointed and tired-emotionally and
physically.
I'm done
Spiritually, I'm gaining strength-my faith is strong.

I just don't know what to do anymore at times like
this
This is a part of you- I'm not into it.
I know I don't deserve this
You are struggling with demons you can't seem to
win.
Life is short
You need to give me more.
2/7/20

I PULLED AWAY

I pulled away
Knowing how you felt and feeling like it needed to
be this way.
Feeling like you needed space
Wanting to respect your choices because I care
about you and I respect your heart, brain and
faith.
So, I pulled away
Because it hurt to know the changes when we
now share space.
I've always known we had our differences
They never mattered the way they matter now
during a pandemic.
As the rules and guidelines changed, so did we
As we made choices and stand our ground-
somehow that meant the relationship started
dwindling.
Differences in opinions and beliefs, now meant we
show up differently
Differences in choices now meant not creating
new memories.
I've never felt so close and yet so far from you
I've never felt so hurt and yet so accepting too.
Every thought I once thought and said "would
never be"

Now it's all reality.
9/24/21

ME AND HER

sometimes I want to pull my hair out
my daughter loves to try to "call me out "
anytime we get into arguments or anytime she
gets in trouble
she likes to play and back talk but I don't like back
talk and we clash
our birthdays are 5 days apart so I am sure we are
very similar and maybe that's chaos at times

We both want fairness and to prove a point
Which many times we clash- this can't succeed for
us both

she likes to say in anger
"Your groups aren't working"
"Show your groups the real you"
"Let me tell them how you really are"
"Tell them how you are mean"

I am mean sometimes
I am not a perfect mom
I am not a perfect wife or human

428

Truth is I am all these sides of me
Truth is, my "mean side" doesn't come out in my
"groups"
I am a different teacher than mom
But being a mom helps me be a better teacher
And being a teacher helps me be a better mom
And these groups are helping me find me, love me,
grow me
And I love showing up- with whatever is real for
me in that moment

I am a grown up, I know feelings can be big to
handle
she is also smart and knows how to try to hurt and
upset me
I also know those feelings can be very real in the
moments

---today she wanted to finally talk things out right
as I was starting a zoom meeting and so she
refused to leave
I refused to miss my zoom
so, she joined. she joined meditation and book
reading by Barb Klein and everything read was

right on point for us both and it's so crazy how
everything always aligns and timing is so right

I am so thankful for the soul care group and zoom
and people and hope to one day be in a space
with everyone off the screens

I am sitting with so much healing and gratitude
and motivation and love and support

**this group makes me feel proud to say things
out loud
to really share my soul and feel safe and powerful
and supported
I am thankful for that

I am grateful to show up in my confusion and
crazy, and real feelings with myself and my
daughter-with my daughter and that the space
helped us both

I am so thankful for it all
I am sitting with so much positive energy

MONDAYS MATTER

mental health matters

self-care matters
owning what's real, releasing tears, sharing your
heart and hearing others-it all matters

this group is a life-line
these women are beyond amazing

one day, we will meet
I am holding that vision and us all as wonder
woman or whoever empowers you and makes you
feel good
10/5/20

SAND
I drew that line in the sand
how am I here again?
I made it out before
but here I am once more.
the sand gets in my eyes, in my shoes and my
clothes
I dig my feet deeper in the sand, into the
unknown.
feet on the ground, is all I know
feet in the sand, feels like home away from home.
the wet sand is held together a bit more

still easily broken, but more molded for sure.
I drew that line in the sand
but the water washed it away
how am I here drawing it again?
why am I drawing what won't stay?

thank you Jeannette Kuilan-Mejias for those first
two lines.
I needed to feel those feelings, acknowledge
them, tap in and release. Thank you for sharing in
our soul group and help heal the souls of others-
well, you sure are helping mine. I feel happier.
even if in the moment.
10/6/21

July 24, 2020 ·
I just don't know why you didn't say no
So many reasons I'm sure, so many - I know.
I just don't know why you didn't say no
You were sober, you had control.
You didn't want it enough, the life without it.
You wanted it too much, the life with it.
I wish you would've said no
You knew you'd be asked but you said you'd say
no.
I am so thankful you made it home

You will never be alone.
These choices tear us apart
It's not that it makes loving you hard.
But it does hurt
I keep praying for the tools that will work.
I am learning how to take control of my reactions
and thoughts
I am allowing myself to feel, I'm not saying I'm not.
But I'm choosing to no longer repeat
It's a thin line between recovery and defeat.
We are indeed a team
But we also have our own journey, our individual
story.
I love who you are when you are your best self
I know you can be even more but you have to
want it for yourself.
I am thankful for your life
I am thankful to be by your side.
Even in the hard times
I am learning every time.

You get another chance to say no
And I'm just thankful

Fun filled Friday,
Freedom to choose,

Fears are real,
Feel the feels,
Fill up your tank,
Finish that task,
Fight or flight,
Fix what you can,
Faith over fear,
Flowing not forcing

ESSENTIAL WORKER

All essential workers need more love and support
Essential workers are just people, living life the
best they can- working hard
Everyone has different journeys, life happenings
They are dealing with extra hard work
environments and expectations and danger with
this pandemic
Some are battling addictions
Some lost loved ones
Some have children
Some have marriage or spouse things to work
through
Some have lack of sleep
Some have loved ones fighting battles
Some are in fights about custody or visitation or
rights

434

Some are battling poverty, body image, shaming,
blaming, negative talk, bullying, suicidal
thoughts....
Some are healing from things that aren't discussed
Everyone can use counseling, self-care, self-love,
sleep, more money, days off....
My heart really hurts for all those fighting battles
we do and don't see
Mental health is so important.
So extremely important.
Check on your loved ones, on your friends, your
family, your coworkers, your people.
We are all we got and we are all holding so much
7/12/20

CURFEW

Something about having to be in now
Makes me want to be out
Curfew.... never had a curfew before 👀
6/1/20

LENA

I wanted to stick to the space provided here, in my
mother's quest print out- knowing if I used my
notebook I would write forever.
For the first time I am really thinking of me, Lena.
Not me the mom or teacher or wife.
But me and I realized I have been holding myself
back from goals and dreams.
My want to do everything as a family and team
and to support others in living their best life has
meant putting me and mine to the side.
Forever I have said and felt what makes me happy
is making them happy, being together, making
memories.
But now, as I still feel that- I have shifted.
I am thinking of me. Me before the title of mom,
wife, teacher- and I am going from there....
it's all new, to think of me in this way. To put me
first, without extra attachments.
But I am giving myself permission to find me and
be me and do me- knowing that will still be what's
best for us all
Grateful for today's second session in mother's
quest spark your e.p.i.c life series. Summer 2020
5/31/20

SELF-CARE

I have come to believe that caring for myself is not self-indulgent, caring for myself is an act of survival" Audre Lorde.

I just saw this and wow. yes, this is where I am at. This is where I have been stuck for many years. As a parent, a partner, a daughter, a caregiver.

not wanting to leave anyone out, not wanting others to be let down or fall behind, not wanting to hurt feelings and wanting to experience moments together.

"You have to put the oxygen mask on yourself first in order to help others"-this has stuck in my head for years. It is something I have been intentionally working on and now am shifting into way of being.

today I was honored to be a part of Mother's Quest Spark Your E.P.I.C. Life Series!! This is my 3rd time but each experience has been different in so many ways. I am so excited and loving the experience already. I love meeting new people, learning about new people, learning about familiar people, championing others and continuously finding myself.

I am on a quest for so much, finding a new peace has been big on my mind and heart and soul and I

have been on the path for years and its coming to
be with support, intention and flow.
I am on day 2 of the 21-day abundance.
day 1 of this new cycle and series of mother's
quest.
and I have so much more to look forward to.
thankful grateful blessed
5/24/20
May 22, 2020 ·
I had to go to the bank today.
on my walk back a woman asked if I had any
change. I said sorry no, as I checked my pockets.
she went on saying how long she has been
homeless. she was in a wheelchair.
I continue to walk quickly to catch the light.
but I start pulling out my wallet because I know I
have a dollar; I think I do. and I did. I turned back
around and gave her two dollars.
as I was walking, I said out loud "thank you dad"
tears start forming. this all while I was thinking at
how I became this person. this person who easily
says no when I used to be the person who would
always say yes and try to help.
somewhere in my life people made me feel it
wasn't ok to help. that giving my money would
just go to addiction or something I wasn't ok being

a part of. that I didn't want to support people's bad habits. I didn't want to help someone to their grave or anything horrible. and I really did not want to be lied to because my heart is a giving heart and it does not need a lie to be on the receiving end.

all my life growing up that was me, giving. help who asks, who needs it.

for the past few years, I have lost that part in me, when it comes to certain situations. I let pain and other people's opinions change my heart and ways. I let bad experiences mold me differently. I started fighting this part of me because others said I was "too nice" and I have been searching so hard how to find a balance between that me and the one who also wants to be ok with who people are and okay with space when something or someone doesn't serve my life, its ok to not be a doormat or used...to find that balance.

I remember telling my dad why did you give that guy so much money, he is just going to buy alcohol or something.

my dad said, if that's what he is going to buy, he was going to get it with or without my help. that guy was me before and I have found my way. I know how it feels to be that guy. someone can choose to do so many things to get what they want, if someone is asking for help and I can give it-why not. someone once helped me. we all find our way.

that forever changed me. even if I didn't change. I remember when I was young someone told me they wanted money because they were hungry. I was a child; I had no money so I grabbed food from inside. I remember watching to see how happy they would be to eat but the person threw it in the trash. I remember thinking, I wasn't good enough, I couldn't help, that person lied to me-I remember feeling angry and hurt.

today I found that spark of that "old me" with a balance of me now.... I had 3 dollars...I gave 2....me today still watched her reaction.... she said "thank you, god bless you" and I said "god bless you" that felt amazing. it hit me in all of the right ways. it was meant to be.

I literally had made a post earlier today and many days about the homelessness all around us...

But we can't just see it or talk about it. We need to do something

thankful, grateful, blessed

I wanted to write about this right when it
happened but life got me distracted and then
boom-more signs and memories and growth....
I had to explain this experience before I can get
into what unfolded for me even more recently
...because, it does all connect...it all always
connects
May 22, 2020 ·

my intention has been to find my "zen" and learn
new practices that will help me achieve some
more/new peace
faith over fear
flowing, not forcing
May 15, 2020 ·
I am many things.
who am I?
I am a writer, teacher, mom, photographer, care-
taker. I am honest, thoughtful and a poet.
I am on a quest for making changes: creating the
environment that brings me peace.
I am on a quest to treat myself with the same love,
care and support I give others.
I am on a quest to level up.
Mom, teacher-will always be me. But now I want
the title of coach. I have been a coach before, but

now- to level up-to a new me.... a life coach and to define what that would look like for me.

I am on a quest for change.

intentional and actual.

I even see me writing those books I have always seen myself doing. And maybe that comes first to help me become the coach I want to be...

Cheers to figuring it all out... or letting it happen without "figuring it out"

time to make it happen

April 30, 2020 ·

it's not always easy to do but I hope you find the courage to put yourself first

treat yourself as good as you do others

listen to your body. hear it and take action.

get support. ask for help.

love yourself the way you love others.

say yes. say no.

do what serves you. let go of what doesn't.

and always be thankful.

count your blessings and face your challenges with patience.

its ok to be real, feel and move forward.

and its ok to be transparent.

saying goodbye to April.

FEEL THE FEAR AND DO IT STILL

you might hear my voice shake
courageous conversations take being brave.
feeling the fear and doing it anyways
feeling the fear and saying it anyways.
it's taken me a long time to learn how to stand up
for myself
to speak my feelings even if it's against someone
else.
I am not speaking to fight or be given what I want
I am speaking to be heard, to be understood.
I stand for fairness, I stand for equality
I know sometimes we argue because we feel the
same but differently.
I may be leaving with sweat stains, a recovering
shaken voice
but I am leaving proud to be heard and to feel I
have a choice.
I wouldn't call this confrontation
I would call it a type of conversation.
questions asked and answers
feelings shared
thoughts shared.
validation, confusion, frustration,
definitely a situation
it had to happen.

and sooner better than later
now it's out the way
and we can move on.
we can move along without right now tainted any
more than what it is.
we can move on and let this be of the past.
it is so hard to be brave.
it is so hard to be seen.
it takes courage to be brave.
it takes confidence to speak to be heard.
but it only takes seconds of courage to make a
whole different outcome.
and even if it's hard to feel and deal, you can be
proud that you did it.
whether you get what you want or not.
be proud of what you accomplished.
because just speaking up is an accomplishment
and sometimes so is being silent
whatever your accomplishment is, be proud of
that
whatever courage looks like to your-own it.
10/31/20

Give it up
I want a soda
I told myself to give it up this week

So, I picked up doing other things like drinking
juice
So now I'm telling myself that's just as bad, so why
not have some soda
Everything is bad for us
Do it in moderation, that matters right?
I gave up soda because of how much I was
drinking it
And because I want to feel different.
I want to be healthier
I want to feel better.
I also need to put my phone down
I keep picking it up for no real reason
No real intention
Just to be scrolling
Just to add to my mind so much that's going
wrong
Taking in all the positives
Trying to spread some positivity
Constantly taking screen shots to share
Some I do and some I don't
It keeps my mind a mess
So, I erase it all, clearing my phone and vision of
the madness
Clearing the energy constantly
Wanting to be real, wanting to heal

and wanting to rest to restore to continue to do
the work
Telling myself the things I come across is for a
reason
Trying to learn the lessons
Trying to find my purpose
Wanting to be of service
Wanting to be my best self
So that I can help
I want a soda, but I don't need it
I can go without it
Is this addiction?
What if we change our thinking around
addictions?
What if that's just a story we tell ourselves
It's just another substance that gives different
reactions
Different distractions
What if it doesn't matter and we tell ourselves the
story can change
What if recovery means healing and that it's for
anything?
What if today my mind-set changes
About the person loving an addict
And being the one with an addiction

What if we all just focus on healing from our
traumas
But realize traumas don't have to carry negative
emotions
We are all lifelong learners
We are all leaders
We are all capable of being our best self
We are all capable of changing our stories
We all matter
We all have a purpose
All these thoughts and feelings from wanting a
soda
Wanting to make excuses to make it ok
Also realizing excuses and explanation and choices
don't have to be negative
What if we decided nothing was wrong?
What if we just lived to enjoy life
What if we just changed our thoughts to change
our actions
I swear all of what I'm experiencing is in total
alignment
I'm constantly reaching a higher self and I am
loving how it feels
These moments of awakening are everything
Hello Saturday
Hello new day

Thankful for life and all its giving me
All it's showing me 💕✨🌿
Thank you, LORD, thank you coaches, thank you
universe, thank you family and community
7/25/20

BEING HUMAN IS MESSY

I'm seeing so much hurt and confusion these days.
Families and friends being torn apart.
*You can't come with us because you don't have
the shot...
But you can hang with me at home.
Just not around my friends ...
*You can't come over because you don't have the
shot
*You don't have the shot, that's ok it's your
choice. I don't agree but I got it so I'm fine, we can
be around each other
*I have it but don't want my kid to have it
* I have it because I want to travel, or keep my job,
or be accepted, or felt pressured
Whatever the reason.
* I believe in it, it works
But only works if we all do it.
*I can't take it, for whatever reason.
*I can't take it, but wish I could.

448

You should be thankful you can.
* I don't have the shot but you do. We can't spend time; I don't want you shedding on me.
*I had the sickness; I don't need the shot.
*I had the sick and the shot, will get the boosters.
* I got the shot but won't get the boosters.
*I'm waiting for my kids to get the shot and then I will feel more protected.
*I'll hug you and be with you as long as my friends with shots can't see us spending time.
****

Let's add this shot to our deal breakers
Like many do with racism, sexism, sexuality,
status, health options
Let's dive and spread hate and hurt because we
are different in our choices, beliefs, experiences
and truth
Is this really happening?
Yes, it is
It's not new
This part is just "new"
Showing peoples truths and fears and humanity
It's ok.
It's ok to not be ok
To be confused, to be hurt, to be scared, to be
patient and to be different

It's ok to make your own choices and follow your heart
It's ok to change your mind
It's ok to believe differently
I don't think it's ok to bully others just because you came to a choice - you either did or didn't want to make
I don't think it's ok to bully, period
I get sad for so many
I try to remind them what I've had to learn, before the pandemic came to be
"We are only in control of ourselves "
"We have to let others live in their journey; their stories don't have to be ours"
You have to find your peace
You have to find your happy
Because stress is a killer
Mental health is real
And being human is messy
10/8/21

MY CHOICES

my choices are my choices.
although others may base their choices on mine.
I do not feel like my choices are consequences in that way.

450

if anything, my choices bring more clarity.
my choices bring me more peace, even though
some things have changed in ways I never would
have wanted.

your choices are not mine.
your choices are yours, even if you say you are
basing them off of mine.
I will not take responsibility for your choices.
your choices are not mine to carry.

the way you treat me because of my choices, I do
not have to like.
I respect your differences. and our similarities.
the way I treat you, will always be with respect.
even if that means distance because of
differences.

I am thankful. to be where I am wanted and to not
be in spaces where I am not.
I am thankful for support despite differences.
I am thankful for love that has no conditions.
I am thankful for honesty.
I am thankful for life.
12/5/21

AND SO, IT IS

Writing this next book has been a challenge for me.
Yes, I have so much of the content already.
"Pandemic Poetry and reflections" is about my journey the last two years.

why has it been hard to write and complete this book?
every day I say "today will be the day I finish" then today becomes tomorrow and repeat
so many of those same thoughts and fears, just like the first time of writing my first book
"But what makes me important enough to tell my story?"
"Will people want to support me again?"
"Who am I to write this story?"

this book was actually not the one I came into 2021 thinking I was going to complete but a couple of months ago it came to my mind and heart and hasn't left me.
I keep making new dates, I thought it would be my birthday gift to me.
I thought I needed my birthday to hype up sales and love and support and interest, then as that

date passed- I thought I lost my chance at the best possible outcome.

going through journals and posts, once again
feeling like I don't want to leave anything out
and I also want to get it done
what is enough?
what is too much?
can I be me? Can I be seen?

I am writing this book for me.
because I want this moment in time to look back on.
because if social media goes down again or away, then what?
because if I have a story to tell, then maybe others can relate.
I am writing this book because it is on my heart.

Today I was on the phone telling someone about what it was about.
It's about my journey. It's about good things happening to me, in a time when the world was falling apart. It's about having guilt of good things happening to me and knowing I needed to allow myself to embrace the good- because if I could

take care of me then I could show up in the world
a healthier version of myself and in return I would
be putting good into a world that could use more
good.
thank you to my friend Natalie, for asking me
what this next book is about and for hearing me
and reflecting to me that "we all have our seasons"

I still have a deadline. I want to get this done and
send the final copy to tiny book course by the
2oth so I can be in their next photoshoot.
I have a lot to get done.
like, finish writing.
I finally have a cover in mind.
I know I will pay someone from fiverr to format
the manuscript and also create the cover with my
pictures.
I know I want to buy bulk ISBN's

I have work to do. I have this goal I want to
complete for this year to feel better for me.
I know I have done more than enough already but
my soul wants this.

and so, it is
12/5/21

454

PUT ME IN SPACES...

Put me in spaces to take candid photos
That will one day be held dearly as loved one's
pass
Photos that will become gifts for celebrations and
to help with grief

Put me in spaces that allows genuine interactions
Where I can always be me and in return help
others feel the permission to be fully themselves

Put me in spaces where others want to see me
win
Others want to help me level up
Put me in spaces where I am thought of, even
without being there
That I connect with others so deep, that they
speak of me in the best ways even without me
there

Put me in spaces where I feel safe
Where comfort is found in facing fears
And safety is felt even while feeling challenged

Put me in spaces where my faith is elevated

Where my spirit can thrive

No-matter the spaces, I will be reflective
I will be honest
I will write
I will share
I will have gratitude

Put me in spaces and places where I can be
Where I can be me
Where I can be heard and seen - and I don't even
mean by being center stage or anything
I was just sitting in the car reflecting. Writing here
as it came
12/5/21

YOU ARE ENOUGH, RIGHT NOW

On the road earlier today, all that was on my mind,
while listening to the radio
Is- why aren't those I know on the radio?
So many rappers, singers, poets in my feeds that
are worthy

So many coaches, healers, entrepreneurs, authors,
teachers, artists—- in my community spaces

I just want to "make it"
So that everyone else can make it

I want to put everyone on platforms they deserve.
I want to help them get in the rooms and spaces
that will help level them up

I wish we didn't have to work so hard to feel
valuable
It truly takes the right connection to make shift
happen

Pay for your friend's merchandise
Uplift your community
Promote yourself
Promote your loved ones

There's space for us all to "win"
We all deserve to "live"
12/5/21

COMING BACK TO ME

It has been a hard few months for me
with physical pain, family hardships and feeling
lack and scarcity.
as much good as I have going on

457

feeling those hard times, has really been tough.
I found myself spiraling in pain and depression
I found myself back to where I was two years ago-
in that story and mindset.
and although the truth is true
I can't not know, all that I do.
and I know, that this doesn't have to be my reality
I know I can create the change I want to feel and
see.
but I won't lie- the hard stuff has been getting the
best of me
as much as I find gratitude with ease, the good
wasn't feeling like ease to me.

I am slowly coming back to me
aligning daily.
slowly making little changes
because doing everything at once, isn't realistic.
but as I make choices, one by one
I feel like I am more at home.

I do not have to wait for a new year in order to
change
I do not have to wait for a holiday or birthday to
celebrate.
Every day is filled with wins

every moment is a moment to begin again.
12/9/21

MAYBE, YOU LEAVING...
Maybe you leaving means see you later and not
goodbye
Maybe you leaving means I do t have to cry
I can be sad but still be happy for you
You can be right here and I can already miss you
Maybe you leaving doesn't have to mean a break
on making memories
Maybe it means I'll travel this time, maybe it
means what we can't yet see
Maybe it none of this has to mean anything
Maybe life is just life, as it is- not how we think it
should be
Maybe you aren't the one leaving, even though
you are driving away
Maybe it's me who's gone- even while I stay
12/8/21

DON'T LIVE IN MY PAST

I think some people live in my past
Those feelings I use to harbor, no longer exist.
I do get sad with grief at times
But I live a different life.

I have made peace with my dad's transition
I even use new language around the whole
situation.

You see my pause or gather myself and may think
I'm struggling
I am just using the tools that help me.
I may share my story of feelings that feel
unresolved
But truth is, I'm in a better place than I was.

I think some people live in the feelings of my past
They can't see me as evolved from that.
I won't say I'm healed completely
But I am not the same me when grieving.

I have my moments, we all do
I am human, just like you.
You may see tears fill my eyes
You may even hear me cry.

And I don't mind if you want to talk
If my words or faces, brought some stuff up.
I don't mind conversation
But, please don't project your situation.

I am trying to protect me
I don't want to carry what's not mine to carry.
I have taken a long time to get to where I am
To re-wire my brain, to have new perspective.

I think some people live in my past feelings
Sometimes I re-visit them as well but I'm no longer suffering.
I'm living and growing with the moving pieces
I'm learning to teach from my experiences.
I am learning what my stories have taught me
I am figuring out who they help me be.
12/8/21

C19

This day last year
C19 was in our home
We all didn't test
We all had different symptoms
We quarantined from the rest of the world.
We made our own manual and healing
It wasn't your typical positive test day

A year later, I think the long haul is still real
I believe in antibodies
I've never had to test yet

Only 3 out of 6 of us have "had" to (once each)

A year later, rules and fears and life still continue
to change
We still school from home (3 out of 4)

C19 has made its rounds in our loved ones, both
shot and without.
Both recently and not.

What a journey it's been.
12/7/21

SONYA

For the first real time, I allowed that door to open.
I allowed myself to participate. I allowed myself to
be real in the experience

my cousin Sonya said she had some messages for
me.
I listened mostly. It was hard for me to talk when
she wanted me to just speak. It's been a long time,
that we have connected and you haven't been
ready but your dad says you are ready.

kiss? feather?

your dad is playing a song on repeat, did you guys
listen to a song?
go back on your heritage, family and history.
he wants you to connect with his mom.

what's 2? 2 hours ago? 2 days ago? still curious

he says you have been wondering if he is proud of
you and he wants you to know he is
and that you are doing too much, too much at
once. he is proud you are letting go of control,
when you do it. let it be
he says your book was too detailed in the book, a
little...but he understands you needed to do that

why do I see wings? he's showing me.
is there a new book? a book cover? feather?

get into a better relationship with your guide. your
heritage? native American heritage. have you ever
been to New Mexico? check into it, into Apache?
maybe that's the feather. have you ever been to
Texas? maybe you will learn why you are the way
you are?

you are meant to write books; you found your
soul tribe.

so many people are rushing in for you
who's G? who's initial?
I'm hot
speak your recent accomplishments outside

let the expectations go and allow it to be

you know how to communicate and translate onto
paper.
people will want your help to write their stories.
you know how
you will teach others how to create books
you are a teacher, you will teach how to write and
write your stories
you have detail and emotion 'you can pull it from
others

let it be, let it unfold

when you are unsure with this next book, not
enough- don't go back. let it be- let it unfold. your
goal is to be authentic and raw. your imperfection
is perfection, it's your story line of your book.

more people will come to you for help with
writing.

you are the book.
these are the chapters; all you are living.
don't release too much about you because you are
the book

your people are coming. to you. they will grow
with you. whoever you allow.
believe in what you are putting out there. don't
feel lack.
others trust in those who are authentic.
****

I can't make sense of it all now

*Is G for my middle name Guadalupe? who am I
named after?
Is G for Gabbi, who I connected with earlier today
over my dad

*Is two for 2 days ago? when I decided on the
cover of my book. a photo of a dove, from his
funeral. I did not tell a single soul that this cover is
the one I have decided on.

*7, that's today, my dad's favorite number, it's the
1 year of my first book

*I have been doing lots of ancestry DNA, family
trees, digging through pictures and posts and
asking questions of family
I want to know more about me, my bloodline, my
family, my heritage.
I want my kids to know more

*I do wonder if he is proud. I worry sometimes.

*I had a feather I used to keep on my desk that got
misplaced in the switching of rooms. I feel like
feathers connect me to my heritage and roots and
dad

*Just before this call someone dropped off an
envelope to me "a few pages of my book I am
working on, I want you to read and tell me what
you think"

I have had 4 people sign up for the tiny book
course because of my experience

I have had people ask if I would lead a group in how to create books and self-publish

I coached someone through overwhelm, during the course

many have reached out to me, wanting to write a book of their own thanks to me sharing

I did not really agree or disagree to any of it. I just allowed it to be. I let anything that made sense, to make sense and didn't try to force anything that didn't. I was still a bit resistant at times. But I am so grateful for the time and my cousin. A couple things took me by surprise and most of it felt like reassurance 🖤🖤🖤🖤

12/7/2

EXPECTED EXPECTATIONS

We give ourselves expectations we expect others to have of us

We think we know and we take actions based on a thought.

"I can't take time off work"

"They won't understand "

But come to find out, they care more

They are human too and understand
I am no good at work if I am a mess
I am better at work, after taking time to deal with
this
Not only did my boss understand, but drove me to
where I needed to be
I didn't know about bereavement time, I wasn't
ready for this kind of grief

"I just need a day" I remember thinking
I'll be back to work tomorrow.... What was I
thinking?
He never got better, everything happened so fast
I needed way more time- now I was cashing in on
sick and vacation

"I can't have a break to break
Because I need to be a mom, a wife"
I need to live life
Do you know what that's like?
To have all these "shoulds" playing in your mind
And yet it doesn't matter at the same time

when life is taken
And your life is now different
And you no longer feel whole

Because now you are broken

You have to move different
I don't drink or smoke so that outlet is not for me
If I chose that now, it might be the end of my
story

I need to write, document
Feel it and be real
I need space, I need time, I need reflection and
help

I have to take each day and moment as they come
That's the only way for this process to be done

This journey is never ending
I will be forever be coping

People who don't understand, can't
There's no fix it for grief
There's no timeline for healing
There's no cure for this

Grief is grief
You have to take it as it is
Make the best of it? Can't make sense of it

It's a big issue that people are expected to be
anything other than human
Trauma is trauma
Pain is real
Grief is a big deal

Mental health matters
Let it all matter

Because it does

.... It's ok to not be ok
Some people don't know how to handle that
Some people don't know how to respond to
someone who isn't ok
Not being ok isn't a crime, it isn't a disease or
illness (I get it can have factors that do exist)
But grief is grief
It can be heavy
Not being ok doesn't mean something is wrong
with you
Not ignoring your pain, choosing to feel your
feelings- doesn't make you "different or difficult
or weird or a problem"
And I'm that same breath.... It's ok to be ok

No one gets to tell you how sad you have to be,
how fast you need to "get over" anything or when
you should be healed
No one gets to tell you how to feel

I encourage you to allow help, seek help, find
healthy ways to cope and to know you aren't
alone.
12/7/21

NATALIES IDEA
It's Tuesday morning.
Sunday evening Natalie brought up the idea of us
interviewing each other. We are both self-
published authors.
we agreed, we would set a future date to do it.
then, this morning as I was thinking of my 1 year
publish date tomorrow- I messaged her and said
what about interview tomorrow?
we then decided today...which turned to right
now....
we took 10minutes to put on earrings, makeup
and hop on zoom, during her lunch break.

It was that simple! two friends, two authors, two
teachers, two people ----who are helping each
other network.
helping each other grow.
helping each other learn and tell our stories.

we both asked each other questions that the other
loved.
no rehearsal, no time for re-dos.

we can edit and snippet and share what we
please.
there's beauty in recordings.
I still have to learn how to do all of that
but, for now---here it is---in all of its realness and
beauty

I share this to say...
it is easy to support each other
to celebrate each other
to uplift each other
to network
to help each other grow

it didn't take much time at all, to connect and to
show up and to share.

472

I now get to add this to my list of what made 2021 great.
I got to interview someone.
I got to be interviewed.
I put a little makeup on, embraced my natural curls and hair.
I got to talk about something that's hard for me, take deep breaths, smile and live in the moment.
we embraced the moment, the unpolished realness and flowed with it.
I am so thankful.
12/7/21

INQUIRING MINDS WANT TO KNOW

I am very curious about how people feel about using their space/voice/platform to support others?

as in- do you need a fair exchange?
does someone have to meet certain criteria?

what does it take to share someone on your page?
in your business?
on your podcast?
for an interview?

on your Instagram or Facebook?

I guess I am asking because It's been on my mind. Last year as I became a self-published author, many came to me and asked if I would like to share in their groups, I was in. Many came to me offering me opportunities to share in their spaces. I wasn't ready then, and even now sometimes I am not ready- I didn't see what they saw. I didn't feel worthy or "credentialed" enough. but these days I say yes more. Because what an honor to be asked to share my story. what a blessing, to have someone see something in me that they feel like is worth sharing and offering their space for.
I wish I took those opportunities last year, but- it just wasn't a part of my story to say yes at those times, I guess.
Do I have regret? I guess a little. But I also have learned, I have learned I still do not know what it takes to feel worthy. I still get surprised and shocked when people come to me with offers. but now, I say yes. because- I don't have anything to lose. and I have learned from the past.

I have been blessed to be a guest on a podcast this year.

People have purchased my book and shared on
their personal pages.
some have written me reviews.
I am beyond thankful

but this is not about that.
It really just is a question, a curiosity.

over the weekend. a friend, a fellow teacher, a
fellow author. Reached out to me and brought of
the idea of interviewing each other to share on
our platforms, to help each other as self-published
authors.
I have never interviewed someone before, it felt
intimidating because I didn't feel "credentialed" to
have such a role.
but I said yes and we said we would get to it in the
future.
well, morning came today, and the idea came to
me that maybe it would be nice to step into this
fear and excitement and growth as a celebration
for my 1 year of being published as of tomorrow. I
asked her, she said yes---why wait till tomorrow-
lets interview each other today.
I had all the thoughts of: I am a fan of hers, how
could I be worthy to interview her?

how did I become lucky enough to be interviewed
by her?
who am I to do this?
but-----we did it.
I am not expecting anything. I wasn't looking to
share my story. I wasn't looking for this in this
way, or any way. But it came to me, to us and we
rolled with it.

I share this to say----you don't need a podcast or
business or anything to share your story.
you don't need "credentials" or degrees or titles to
network with each other.
we all have talents, gifts, stories- we are all
valuable because of who we are and what we
have to share.

support your friends' businesses.
embrace being an entrepreneur.
embrace who you are.
embrace your life, tell your story-in any way to
whoever you feel.

network-with people. we are all just out here
trying to live life the way that brings us happiness
and fulfillment

476

cheer each other on, see each other, celebrate
each other, support each other.
support and love can look like so many things
these days.

a conversation, a phone call, connecting with
others, sharing with your following, liking/loving a
post, word of mouth of your experience and
personal feelings, buying merchandise--- whatever
it looks like.

thank you, Natalie, for this morning's zoom call.
For the idea and opportunity to interview each
other and who knows what will come from it but
so much already has.
I appreciate you; I value your time and heart.
and I am inspired constantly.
12/7/21

VISION AND LIVE IT

We don't have the money to buy matching
dressers for the boys.
For black Friday there wasn't a sale for the one we
wanted.

last night I was tempted...to charge the credit card
yet again, without knowing how we will pay it off
or when.
But I was tempted again.
Because I have a vison for the life I want to live.
I know it's not all about looks and things.
But when I see what doesn't serve and what could
possibly make life more pleasant, especially as we
are all home a lot more these days.... every day, all
day.
I want our environment to be pleasing, to bring us
happiness, joy and peace and if that means getting
new things that help bring ease and beauty. then
that's what it means.

last night after adding to cart, I took it back out.
It's just not priority.
but waking up, it was still on my mind and heart.

we had searched free spaces. truth is we didn't
find anything and also, sometimes you can't just
settle- because it still may not be the look and
vibe you want.

so, today I pressed order. On that desk and
dresser thing for the boy's room to help create the
look and feel for them they want.

and to my surprise, this dresser thing was not just
a few dollars cheaper, but $20 coupon was
applied.

you can't tell me the universe doesn't work in the
best ways.

I don't need to figure out how or when, right now.
I just need to align and take meaningful action.
I just need to lean in faith and walk in faith.
scarcity mindset does not serve me, it is not
protecting me in the ways that I once felt like I
needed.

It all starts at home; how many times have we
heard that?
It all starts with ourselves.
well, I am working on me.
I am working on we; we are working on we.
we are working on home.

✦we have the power to change our stories

to reframe our thoughts
to live the life, we love
we have the ability to heal
To heal from within, to heal old traumas, heal
open wounds, care for ourselves as we are
To heal our stories
To write our future and create our past from here
on out
we are capable of change, growth, new
beginnings and letting go and saying no
we are deserving- to say yes to what matters and
live in our truth
12/7/21

HEAL FROM WITHIN

I already know what I feel like, When I don't apply
myself fully
I already know what life feels like for me
When I lay in pain because fear of moving has me
not moving
I already know yoga will help
The pain is already real, it's already felt
I already know what chiropractic care has looked
like for me
I know it benefits; I know what it means to let
health be priority over money

I already know how easy it is to spiral into old
stories
But now I know, those stories don't have to be
It's easy to fall into depression
To let that old hurt and negativity in
To lean into the reality that is filled with realistic
challenge
To feel like I have to accept it, because it is what is

But I already know I can create change
I know how it feels to be without pain
I know the tools I have in my tool belt
I know I believe in prioritizing mental health
I know what I have stopped been doing recently
I know it all may be what's affecting me
All I can do is try change again
Get back to what worked before and see what
happens

Cause I already know, what it's like - to not
To not show up
To not drink enough water or get enough sleep
To not get outside or exercise properly
To not smile, dance and have fun
To connect less with others- it all matters so much

To eat out more
To engage in feeling poor

I already know what the mindset can do
What it will do, no matter what we choose

So, today- I begin again
To create the change I want to see, to heal from within
12/7/21

KEEP ASKING WHY, KNOW YOUR WHY

Today, it starts with waking up at my 6:30 goal time again.
For a while I stopped.
Days got darker earlier, colder.
Most of the kids are home from school, so I don't "need" to be up early.
I started going to bed later, scrolling more at night.

After re-evaluating is this goal and change still for me?
Does it benefit?
Is it what I still want?

I decided, yes.

So, today- day one.
I have many goals but today is just to wake up at 6:30.
Not to have it all figured out or to get up but to wake up.

Because, I want to get to bed earlier. So, I want to start my day earlier.
It's bright out already.
Why wait until the new year to practice, now is perfect timing
Today is just waking up.
But future days can be enjoying uninterrupted time with my husband because he gets up early.
It can be house chores before the house wakes up.
It can mean making time to work out, time for me.
It can mean starting my day with more intention.

Hello, 6:30. I actually woke up at 6, went back to sleep and then by 6:25 decided- I don't need or want to hear my alarm, so I silenced it. But I silenced it and decided I would not close my eyes again. And reminded myself of why...

Because I want to prioritize sleeping better at night

💀sleep is so important. For our health, for healing, for making things happen
🐾building g trust starts with ourselves first.
Changing our thoughts will change our actions
👣we have to start somewhere
Know you why(s)
🖤align with what matters to you
The rest, will fall into place when you continue to be your true self

I'm feeling proud, accomplished, happier and inspired already 🙆
12/7/21

GOD ALREADY QUALIFIED YOU
"You are good enough as you are now! You have substance"

"You don't have to prove yourself. You don't need to research. "

"You are living so much. You have so much experience that can be put on your resume. You do not need degrees or tests or titles"

"You can coach others to write, you already have done that. "

"You have a story to tell Lena"

"I see you with veterans, with people-helping them in their grief.
People can still and should still go to see a counselor and get help.
but- you can also help because of your experience, your story.
you are not prescribing or diagnosing."

"If you've been through it, it's your experience and expertise
but you are not claiming to be an expert
you are using your skills and your life"

"You didn't go to school to be a mom, but you are"

"a lot of people lost loved ones who need you and want to hear you "

4 days ago, Natalie really came through with all
the words, all the truth, all the love.
and she isn't the first to say many of these things
to me.
I keep hearing all of these things. Before I wrote a
book and so much after I wrote my first book.
people in grief are coming to me.
people want me to help them write.
people want me to help tell their stories.
people want me to listen
to hold space for them
to speak
people are coming to me....
and I just never felt "credentialed or Degreed
enough"
I always thought "what an honor, but who am I to
be who you are coming to me to be?"

I am just making my way on this journey.
understanding and embracing, for me are two very
different-pieces......little by little
12/9/21

FLIP THE COIN

When did we stop telling each other the
important things?
At one point in time, we told each other
everything.
When did I no longer become the on you could
share your fears with?
When did I no longer become the one for 4 am
conversations?

Why am I the one you call when you're in need?
When all else fails and you know you can depend
on me.
Why am I not the first to know about the big
celebration things?
When did time with others become priority?

Why is spending time, only made time for after
the partying that comes first
Why does making time for us, have to be so much
work?

It wasn't the pandemic that brought us farther
apart or closer
It wasn't that there's nothing in common, it's just
convenience wasn't any longer

....
What a gift, to be someone you still tell your good
news to
I am so happy I get to celebrate you
In middle school we cared about who was first
/last to be told anything
These days, we are grownups and there's no room
for categorizing

Other people's choices and feelings have nothing
to do with us
We each are in charge of our own actions and
thoughts

What a gift, to be someone you come to - at your
worst of times
To be your safest place, still after all this time
In high school we visioned a dream future
together
Thinking we needed to do it with each other, in
order to make there

But here we are and here we've been, on our own
journeys
Making our way still, to that vision we used to
dream

Life takes us on so many trips
I am so thankful for the experiences
The ones we always get to share
Thanks to technology, we still get to be there
without being there

What a gift, to still be considered best friends
To have become family, the kind that's chosen
12/10/21

MEMORIES AND REFLECTING
I pictured outdoor school for the both of us when
we moved back to alameda in March 2020
As the pandemic hit, I thought "how perfect is this
for me"
I felt like GOD was reminding and reinforcing my
desire to teach, outside /in different ways than
the "normal schooling"
I felt like it was finally time to make time for my
continued education, and the way that could work
because everything was virtual and with so much
chaos and change- everyone was on the same
page for mistakes and grace
But I didn't take Ed any age of online school for
me

Or outdoor school teaching - for her and us
I don't regret but I wish I was able to do it all
However, I've been writing books, self-publishing,
kids are in school while at home, I've been in
coaching groups and now training, I've been living
dreams while in fear and wonder what next
year/future holds for me
What do I want?
Before the pandemic, life happened. Such as the
below post. We continue to have ups and downs.
We continue to grow and change.
Pandemic or not, life is moving along
And time doesn't stand still
But there's time, still
12/10/21
December 10, 2018 ·
Today is a day of heartache, heartbreak and
gratitude.
Today is my daughter Athena's unexpected last
day of infant care. However, for the last 4 1/2 -5
months I have been beyond blessed to be her
teacher and mom. To have her with people I trust.
To not miss out on her growing. To have her apart
of AIA and my dream job. To see her make friends
and family here in this community with adults,
infants, toddlers and high school youth.

My team was given hard news Friday and our AIA
staff received it tonight after our parents/families
of our children. Then our youth in program found
out.
Beyond emotional throughout the ages, races,
faces, positions. I'm thankful for the support, care,
fight, community. Right away my youth jumped
into "how do we help" not hearing this is out of
our control. Our youth who we empower were
told they are powerless. And they didn't hear it,
still determined to find a way for change.
I am proud and sad and so much more.
As an end date is definite, the future is unwritten.
So much beauty through this pain. So much love. I
couldn't be more blessed with the people I'm
surrounded by.
Thank you to my husband for providing us lunch
today and a coworker for providing doughnuts.
The pain in my heart is strong but eventually the
love will be all I remember

WORTHY TO BE ME

I have so much passion, to get so much done
sometimes those fun projects start to not feel like
fun
I think I have been in denial about burn-out

so much good, so much "bad"- and having to
figure everything out.
I have a few things I want, need to get done for
me to be at peace
then I need a break, to just be.

so, I can figure out what's next for me
I miss teaching, I miss "working."
I miss school but not what school is these days
I get the rules but I am not ready for "new normal"
in any way.

I miss being in connection
smiling faces, sickness even.
the world went crashing and I feel like we missed
out on that "reset" as a whole
life for teachers, parents, and students should be
on a better level.
as a world we should be doing better
hustle and burnout are not a badge of honor.

comparing traumas should not be a thing
we should be helping; we should be healing and
uplifting.

as this year is coming to an end

I am not sure where to close and where to begin.
I am not sure what's next for me
I am not sure what's next for "we."

last year, for me was a dream come true
obviously not in the ways that were not but in the
bigger picture- for me it was so much of what I
ever wished could be true

this year, has been blessed but way more stressful
than the last
next year, I am not even sure of the path.

but it's time to get to know me more
its time step in and up-get center.
its ok to lead from behind
but I think it's time to get more into the light.
it's time to try new things
it's time to believe.

I am capable of my dreams
I am worthy, to be me.
12/10/21
December 12, 2020 ·

-You've got people sick, regular sick. Testing to prove they aren't C19 positive, rejoicing in having sicknesses you wouldn't have rejoiced in before.
-people who have allergies or get a cold or whatever- scared to cough or sneeze -fear of being looked at differently
-you have people testing positive being treated like the plague
(You wouldn't know to treat them that way if they didn't share their results)
- you have people testing positive scared to share because of judgment, hatred, guilt, blame- so they don't tell anyone
They live in fear and silence and depression and loneliness
Some continue to live life normal to not be treated differently (and spread the sickness)
-it's like there's no winning in this
- treat others how you would want to be treated
I believe in transparency
And I also get why people hide or lie
And it's not just C19
It's HIV, aids, cancer, depression, lice (yes, whatever the case)

People are scared to accept their realities, scared
to ask for help, scared to share—-because they are
scared to become a label and target
Bullying is real
Fear is real
(Fear is valid) but don't let it make you less kind
Be thankful when others own their truths, share
their truths
Be thankful when others find comfort and safety
in you
Be thankful when others are brave and
courageous
No one has to be
No one "owes" anyone
Be thankful
Whoever you are judging.... could easily be your
situation.
Be careful how you treat others.
What I'm seeing and hearing, is nothing new
It's just new variables to old equations
And I'm praying we work towards different results
I'm hoping we work toward building each other
up- even through differences
Prayers for kindness, understanding, love, support
and making it through 🤍 ✢ 🙏
December 12, 2020 ·

Please check on your loved ones
check on those you care about
check on those you would miss if they were to be
gone
check on people
This week has been eye-opening
with being quarantined
with having a positive result in the house
with going through realities
emotionally, spiritually, physically, mentally
Not everyone reads a Facebook post
not everyone knows how to respond in certain
situations
not everyone can "show" up the way you wish
they would or could or feel
when you are quarantined, especially in your own
home, isolated by masks or rooms or what not-it
can take a toll
please check on those loved ones
adults and kids are affected
some won't care if anyone checks in
and some, really care
some wonder why "their" people who they would
be there for-haven't even sent a text or call or
facetime
depression is real

the world is hard enough on the regular
2020 is crazy enough in itself
check on your loved ones
even if it's a hi or
how are you or
I miss you
or "you have been on my mind"
you don't have to send a gift or food or anything
a simple text or call is more than enough
but if you have a small gesture in you, from the
heart-that works
we are all trying to get through life
trying make ends meet
trying to find happiness and safety in our bubbles
we are all trying to make meaning and
understanding of this year and what's to come
The days have been eye-opening
when I hear my kids wonder why so and so hasn't
checked on them
when I see and hear my husband's phone mostly
going on because of coworkers, where's everyone
he is there for?
when I hear my kids question these things. I think
that is the eye-opening part
and it reminds me how each of us are going
through things we don't know about

we all have our own bodies, minds and hearts and honestly, we don't know what's going on inside each person
so, if you have the capacity to check in. If you read this. I am inviting you to Text or call or facetime the kids, ask how they are-just normal. They miss their loved ones. It doesn't hurt to reach out to the grown-ups as well. We are all human.
sending prayers and love out there. And I do know---the phone works both ways. we all can be better about being there for each other. we all can always be a better version of ourselves.
Hello Saturday. Surrender.
I am so thankful to those who have been here for us, any day and especially this week. I am thankful for community, family, support, love, prayers, vibes, wishes, conversations. I am thankful for life. I am thankful for honesty, for risk, for courage and for hope.

8.11.21
I am perfectly imperfect
It all starts with me
I deserve to look good, feel good and be selfish for me, to show up better for them
I am the right parent for them

And they are the right children for me

Everything in my life is my story,
It has created my journey, and is my brand
My truth is my marketing
I am my business
August 31 · 21
I have really been fighting with myself this month.
I have so much good in my life. Groups,
communities, people and practices.
I have been feeling drained and unsure financially.
I have been trying to take peace in feeling like I
have to "take a break" or press "pause"
When I stop and think of why I started
Why I invested
What these spaces and faces mean to me...
I am clear, why I am "here" - I mean "there"
I hear others not understand
And how can you, if you aren't in it
If you are living this goodness
Being in alignment with yourself
Finding your people, your peace and growth is a
very personal experience
Thank you freedom yoga
Thank you soul care
Thank you courageous life society

Thank you surrendered healing
Thank you mother's quest
Thank you "get it done" and tiny book course
Thank you to all of my coaches
Thank you to everyone in my corner, in anyway
You are much appreciated, valued and loved
Do I want everyone to have these experiences?
Yes
Do I think these coaches and places and spaces
are for anyone? They can be
I believe in the goodness
I also know- you are only ready for, what you are
ready for- when you are ready for it
With that being said- so many "free" and low-cost
opportunities come about. If you ever feel called- I
encourage you to listen to your callings and see
where it may lead.
Thank you for giving me spaces and practices that
have helped me in countless ways. I have met so
many amazing people through each of you. I have
gained "family" and friends and purpose. Thank
you for all you do, how you show up, all you are.
Thank you for making decisions both easy and
challenging in the best ways
September 5 · 21

Finished being a guest on my first podcast.
(WEBS)
My shirt is wet from sweat; my heart is soul-filled.
The alignment is so real
Gratitude is what I feel.

*I have thought, more than often "I wonder what
it takes to be on someone's podcast. I wonder
how successful I have to be, to feel worthy. I
wonder what success even is. I wonder when I will
be important enough for someone to be
interested."

well, not too long ago I made a post about my
dreams and things. Of one day wanting to
podcast, what it means to brand myself when I'm
not so sure....
someone commented that I could totally do a
podcast and should...
then, a soul care sister reached out and said she
would like me on her podcast!

I have learned what it means to not be ready and
that's ok. But I also learned how it feels to miss
out on opportunities that aren't always here later
to redeem.

I didn't want to miss out again, I wanted to face fears, I wanted to have this new experience and see what comes from it.

Someone saw something "good enough" in me to ask me to be on their podcast.
it's not just that, people I admire have asked me to speak in groups I love before and I just was never ready to step up to the plate.
I am not trying to sell myself or the book. I have no script. And that's how I like it.
But I do have a story-and maybe it can help someone. That's it, that's why-that's the reason to speak up. To use my voice, beyond words on paper....to use my voice, to hear my voice, to show up differently.
There's power and magic and so much more in spoken words. In community. In opportunity.

I was always worried to speak up. I am so thankful for the tiny book course virtual book fair this year, where I recorded an audio-sent it in and people listened! That was scary and huge and refreshing. But, that-was a huge stepping stone to help me today.

To use my voice. Even when tears and the shaking
came. Even when the words were lost or took
time to speak.
I am so thankful.

yes, I now think of things I "should" have said.
but I am so excited and anxious to hear episode
46 on Wednesday.
I made new connections, deepened connections
and I am just so proud of me.
I am so thankful for the two beautiful souls I got
to spend time with today. I feel so honored to
have been "worth" their time

forever a life-long learner.
and to whoever needs to hear this----- you are
good enough now
you are more than good enough
you don't have to wait for someone to ask, you
can ask
your story matters, please share it

Today I was even so moved, I even verbally
offered the idea and read out loud some of page
46. Not during recording but to these two
beautiful souls I was able to connect with. I chose

46 because I will be guest on episode 46...and when I opened the page-Wow.
everything continued to align.
September 7 ·
I know I was there; I was speaking. I did speak.
But I don't remember what I said.
I probably jumbled words and messed up on "delivery" of things sometimes.
Of course, later I thought of things I "should have said" or could have said "better"
But that's life, right? We are never "perfect" and we are our biggest critics.
And yet, everything is just "perfect" as is.
But I remember how I felt.
Proud. Nervous. Excited, grateful. Nervous.
No script or notes. Just heartfelt words.

Then this morning I see this beautiful video made.
I watched with my husband, and kids.
Wow. What a way to bring in the day ✨🖤

If you tune in, I will be hearing this for the first time, along with you ✨🖤 tomorrow

I couldn't be more thankful, grateful and overjoyed with my first podcast guest role. Thank you so very much for helping me face fears and make more dreams come true. I had such a beautiful time connecting with you both.

September 8 ·

It's here everyone. Just click the link

Episode 46 is my first guest appearance on a podcast

I have listened through it at 4am my time (nervous at what I may have said wrong or left out)

But even with "what could have been "better""

I am proud

I am thankful for the opportunity, support and connections made

*I had actually been talking to Julie and sharing with her for a while before the tiny book offering

That I wanted to write children's books.

Since teaching I had all these ideas and then more specific something for my mom and family.

But I had to get this grief book out first.

Something about my healing, I needed to do this to move forward. To show I could do this. Dream come true.

Knowing mothersquest was an affiliate

Knowing Julie invited and was doing it- there was a level of trust.
I don't want to miss out, feeling.
Knowing Julie was inviting mothersquest members I was so excited to make connections and be on this "first time" journey with people I admire.

Thanks to groups I'm in and coaches I have like Adelina I now know terms like imposter syndrome. I hear myself talk about weighing pros and cons out, in this episode. Cons don't always have to mean something negative or "bad." It's ok to not be ready.
Its ok to wait.
Its ok to not have the money.
Its ok to sit with a dream and take your time.
but when that "right" time comes, you will just know it.
I just had reached the point where I knew what not doing it was like and I was ready to not regret any longer.
I was ready to turn "incomplete" into "complete"
I was ready to want to feel and live the reality of not giving up

Alternatives in action helped me use my voice
Helped me pursue my passion of teaching
AIA helped inspire me, support me and become
who I always wanted and who I didn't even know I
could be
At AIA teachers are called "coaches" and I always
had people helping me level up. Someone was
always seeing something in me that I didn't really
see in myself, coaches pushed me in the best
ways. They challenged me to reach new parts of
me.

How amazing the kids didn't come in until the end
of the podcast.
Thank you to my children and family for allowing
me the time and space to have this experience, I
was so nervous.
Thank you to my husband and kids for using their
artistic abilities to help create this book.

After this episode I read the first half of page 46
(Barb Klein moment) because she often asks
people to choose a number and will read from her
book. Well, I chose to offer to offer to turn to and
read page 46 because I am on episode 46.
It all felt in alignment

My fb diary turned into a book!

November 19, 2020 ·
* This year with school online has meant we get our oldest every other week instead of just after school Friday-Sunday morning.
It's literally a dream come true.
*This year in march we moved back to alameda, to the house we moved from the march before! I manifested that all last year! you have no idea!
*This year I did not have to pay for mothers quest spark your epic life because I was "grandfathered in" but I paid! I paid to help someone in the future, because someone did that for me before!
*I have invested in the people around who are doing such amazing things with their life.
-Angel's mom is a pure romance consultant and I have ordered from her several times. To support her, to treat myself, to celebrate her wins. She has also gifted me items. (It is so important to lift others up and we did that for each other. It is so important to help each other win. Even if you just like or love or comment on a post. Even if you share) I say this to share. If you want pure romance items, go check her out. Support a mom

working from home. Support women empowerment

-Natalie McDonald Perkins wrote a book and I paid to own it and to have it signed. We went to high school together. "Best In Me"

I say this because I feel so honored to own not just her book, but a signed one!

I think everyone should own this book.

-I purchased Linsay pera's book from the mystics society. That was also signed, I feel so honored. I have never paid so much for a book but I did it because I wanted to be able to hold this book of goodness and so many faces, I admire purchased this book so I knew it was worth it.to my surprise it's so much more than that. You are getting more than just a magnificent book. You get help through it.

-I signed up for inspired possibility series with barb klein, after not being able to afford it previously. I made what I thought was a huge leap of faith- knowing she was a kind woman. I spent money on an experience that was unknown but that I grew to love. I wasn't sure I could join again- knowing I was doing other things financially. Then I was able to pay for a whole year! Thank you barb for all of the payment options. (So many could do what was right for them)

I was drawn to barb because of her poetry, who I "met" through mothersquest

Thank you, Julie, and mothersquest for connections. Thank you barb for sending me your book, for reaching out to me about joining soul care.

-I signed up to be in the courageous life society with Jessica Stong, I invested after being a part of her free 5-day morning makeover.

She gives so much of her for free, the price to pay to join was more than worth it.

I also "met" her through mothersquest/Julie and I am so thankful

-I invested in seeing a chiropractor. 1st for a 3 month, 3 times a week process. and then again! for 20 more adjustments over 6 months with Dr. Heidi wroebel

After years of pain, unanswered questions, prescriptions and a couple of chiropractic visits elsewhere. I finally found what aligned with me. I was finally ready to try something new and really go for it.

-I invested in myself to take the Tiny Book Course with Alexandra Franzen and Lindsey Smith.

I also did this knowing Julie was an affiliate and that this would include mothersquest members (thank you Julie. Because of how highly I think of you, it makes me trust in others when you are the connection) because of your connections, I feel safe to be brave.

-I invested in mothersquest milestone back to school coaching with Julie Neale and at the time it was hard to do financially but we made it work. Thank you, Julie, for always being there for me.

-I say I invested because you have to invest in yourself (financially, mentally, emotionally- time wise- everything) when you put money down- it somehow matters more (to some) it's a type of accountability and you get what you pay for (coaches are out here changing lives and the world and deserve their pay)

-I became a Doterra wellness advocate. I paid to take the course and get a certificate. I am an essential oil specialist, according to the certificate I am a Doterra consultant now, I need to get into that more, once I am done writing my first book and becoming self-published

Like any education- it costs. But it's what you do with it all that truly matters

-I invested in taking part in the first mama medicine with Beth sachnoff- thanks to the scholarship space
thank you to Deja Gould for making that connection
Again- you learn what's worth it and as you learn the value of people and their gifts- it becomes easier.
It's not always "affordable ". Take advantage of free, of scholarships and of opportunities
-I invested in VIP ACCESS to Dr. Elisa Songs Facebook pandemic support. I loved both of her free masterclass
I know with where I am at in life that I can learn so much and feel more at peace with this investment in my "toolbox"
*I did the 21-day abundance challenge with Deepak Chopra thanks you barb Klein
*I was gifted a scholarship spot to join "begin anew mini retreat" Hosted by Barb Klein and Carol Moon
I am so thankful. I haven't been able to join more but that was an amazing experience.
*I joined Beachbod on demand with Lynda Zepeta Gutierrez as my coach and started working out,

started changing my eating, started creating habits, invested in shakeology.
and my chiropractor was also a member!
I would have never before spent that kind of money on me, on a drink, on any of this.
But I am changing. I am learning what I want my investments to look like. I am figuring out how I want to feel and what I want to see as a "show for my money" I am learning what matters more to me, right now
*I now own my first pair of democracy clothing jeans.
So thankful for the discount (through mothersquest)
Have you noticed how much mothersquest is bringing goodness to my life?
I so recommend you join
*I was a part of overcoming overwhelm with Jennifer white. twice!
*I was a part of mommy and me mindset challenge with Cayla craft which was a free 5 day. then she did a free 3-day wealth reset
*All kids are doing remote learning this year and we are loving it. It has been a dream of mine to have them all "homeschooled"
*Sobriety for loved ones has been amazing

*I dipped my feet into being a virtual assistant

*I won a prize in the gratitude challenge and in overcoming overwhelm and in a raffle at the chiropractor, I also won a gift in the morning makeover challenge

*This year my husband and I made 10 years of marriage

*When we moved this year, we gave up having cable, yes even during the pandemic!!!

*I have done meditation and yoga! I haven't created routine yet but I have done them several times

*We have had many bike riding trips since moving back to alameda

*I made it past 1 year of counseling and am continuing

thank you, Native American Health Center

*I tried cbd deep sleep pills and melatonin gummies this year for the first time

In hopes of creating better sleep. I want to prioritize sleep and rest.

*We have supported loved one's business: desserts, foods, masks, decorations, party, shirts-whatever the case

Because that feels better than buying certain things elsewhere.

We are building community, we are strengthening relationships, we are supporting and uplifting each other so that we all can win.

*I completed the book for my mom for Mother's Day, in paper form and want to make it to a real book next, for the world

She loves it and now I see how important that was to get done to lead me to where I am now

*I have gotten rid of lots of stuff and still have lots to go but I am making progress (furniture, things, stuff, food)

*I have had sessions with Adelina "manifest my vision intensive" and got to volunteer with the virtual popup healing center

I went out of my comfort zone

I got even more clarity

*We have used the firepit, spent time with family

*We invested in new furniture that we have dreamed of

*We added plants to the house

*We helped create a garden in the backyard

*We use the dishwasher now and use less paper plates

*We still have both of our moms

*We are seeing things through and taking actions. we are making dreams happen

there is so much good that has come with our 2020.

that does not mean there hasn't been struggle, heartache, pain, hurt, anger, frustration, depression, worry, doubt or fears. Financial struggle is real and so is scarcity mindset. so is victim mindset.

but this post is about the good and I know I didn't list all the good but this is some.

and I know not everyone's year has been or felt blessed, some feel this is the worst year ever, for some- it's hard to see the good and positives through the challenges.

but I try to keep in mind

"Flowing not forcing"

and "faith over fear"

"grace/guilt"

and 2020 being the year of great vision. better vision. self-care, becoming our best selves with the always room to learn and grow.

by focusing on the good, it can only get better. it doesn't mean the other stuff isn't real or present, I'm just manifesting different.

I am working so hard on me. To be better for myself, to show up the way I really want to in the

world, to be better for my family and to have
peace.
I am working on me.
It has been the hardest and best gift
I feel thankful to be able to say I invested so much
of me in/with others because to me that means I
have people I trust; I have people I can count on; I
have people who are special, I have people who
are worth it, I have people who help me reach
higher and higher
When you put money into getting coaching. You
still have to do the work for it to work.
It's not a one-way street. It's not just an exchange.
It's teamwork. It's valuable and so worth it.
Coaches are worth your time, your money, your
support and your dedication.
Just say yes and see where it takes you.
For me, I'm on a roll and can't stop now.
I am constantly inspired, intrigued and "all in."
This post isn't to brag. It's to hopefully inspire. It's
to give gratitude and thanks. This post is to
amplify the good in my life, the share goodness
(resources, create connections)
This post is to say:
you can do whatever you put your mind to
You can make the impossible happen

You can change your story
You can create change
And you can make your dreams reality
This post is to show - don't get scared away from
things because they have a price to pay
Don't let lack of money stop you
Don't let your mindset hold you back
You won't know it's worth it or not
Until you check it out first
"Tell me something good that's happened in 2020"
I wrote all I did because that's my "good"
It's ok to be proud of what's going well
It's ok to celebrate all of your wins (big or small)
These things are really big for me. I have
changed/grown so much
And I am so happy about it
You don't have to give to get
You don't have to receive to want to give
You don't have to share like I do
I don't share for praise or pity
I share because I like to for myself. I like
transparency. I want anyone to know the
greatness out there, I want anyone to know they
aren't alone, I want anyone to know there is a way
to make a way.
If I can help, I will

I love all I get to be a part of and I just want
anyone to know it's all out there for them as well-
you just gotta "try" something "new."

What matters to you?

_____

_____

_____

_____

_____

_____

_____

_____

_____

_____

_____

THANK YOU

I want to take time to share my gratitude and thank you's. Thank you to my husband and children. For supporting me, especially when this journey was stressful but you understood and loved me through it. Thank you for your talents of illustrations and cheering me on.

Thank you to anyone who has cheered me on, who has shared they look forward to the next book and those who have shown me any love on this author journey.

Thank you to anyone who has been here for me, for us- during this pandemic times. For those who helped us when we had covid and those who supported us every other day.

Support looks like so many things. Coaching groups, grocery help, gifts, walks, phone calls, messages, texts, babysitting, honesty, facetime calls and so much more.

Thank you to "open-source wellness." Thank you to my counselor Mila and the Native American health center. Thank you, to all of my coaches during my participation with open-source wellness- thank you Ana (you have done so much for me, for my family and I am cheering you on with your podcast and everything you have going on.)

Thank you, Paul Socket, for the gift of being in "claim your space. "Thank you for offering that opportunity in the overcoming overwhelm challenge. I am thankful I was one of the lucky winners.

Thank you, Barb Klein, for "soul care." Thank you for the space you have created. Thank you for inviting me to join. Thank you for all of the opportunities you share and the space you hold.

Thank you, Julie Neale, for "mothers quest." Thank you for scholarships, for sharing opportunities, for inviting me to be the MC for your virtual birthday party to celebrate you and mothersquest. Thank you for being my mentor, coach and friend. Thank you for work opportunities, thank you for pushing me in all of the best ways. You are where so many ripple effects come from. Because of you and mothersquest I met so many amazing people and have been able to be a part of so many special communities/workshops/groups. Thank you for leading me to Barb Klein, Katie Hannus, Nicole Lee "inclusive life", Lindsay Pera "mystics society", democracy jeans, Jessica Stong and so many more.

-Thank you, Adelina. Thank you for surrendered Sundays, volunteer work, the pop-up-healing event and for surrendered healing gratitude challenges. Thank you for surrendered healing community. Thank you for the opportunity of trade work and being on the dreamteam as the social media connector. Thank you for life mastery and everything else you do. Thank you for connecting me with so many amazing people because of the ways you show up. Surrendered healing has helped me make so many connections with people and places that mean so much to me. Freedom yoga, being one of those places- Kim being one of those people. The dreamteam, being many of those people. Life mastery being another space where I have met new people and connected with some from my past.

Thank you, Jessica Stong, for the "courageous life society" and the opportunity to be a founding member. Thank you for allowing me to be a part of your first group to go through coaching training with you. Thank you for all of the opportunities you have given me-helping me grow in so many ways. Trusting me with roles, I never even saw for myself. Thank you for the virtual assistance opportunities, trade work opportunities, and job opportunities.

Thank you, Kimberly Ky, for "freedom yoga. "Thank you for offering one month of unlimited yoga as a gift/prize during surrendered healing's gratitude challenge. I am so happy I won. Thank you for the opportunity to be Freedom Yoga's ambassador for 3 months. Investing in yoga and being a part of this community has been a dream come true. Kim, thank you for all the love and hard work you do. Yoga has helped with my back pain when I wasn't at the chiro. My kids even joined yoga. Now, my 3-year-old does "cheers" at the end of meetings.

Thank you to my 4th/5th grade teacher and lifelong friend Barbara Schmidtz for bringing poetry in my life and always cheering me on. You have been such a consistent "good" in my life in so many ways. I am forever thankful for your love and support.

Thank you, Alexandra Franzen and Lindsey smith, for "the tiny book course." Thank you, Julie, for inviting me on this journey and opportunity with you and other members of mothersquest. I am thankful to have taken this course, two years in a row now. I am thankful to have been a part of the virtual bookfair and the photoshoot. I have finished 3 books, counting this one. I have become an affiliate and made 4 commissions. I am so thankful for all of the opportunities.

 Thank you, pandemic, for allowing school from home, having our oldest every other week, being able to have the option to work from home, edd, stimulus, covid time off and for all of the opportunities I have been blessed to be a part of. So many coaches offered so many free events and affordable opportunities.

Thank you, Mona, for inviting me to participate in the Shaklee prove it challenge.

Thank you, Lynda fitness, for introducing me to beachbody (that I have now been a member of for two years.) Thank you for the in-person Zumba, that my whole family was able to attend. Thank you for all of the coaching, support and friendship.

Thank you, Jenna Schwartz, whom I met through Julie. I am thankful I won a raffle during mothersquest and landed a spot to join the diveintoporty.

Thank you, Heidi, for doing a pop-up table with me, on my dad's birthday. It means so much to me. Thank you for park days, bubbles, shared snacks, walks just us two and always being a call/text away.

Thank you Dr Heidi Wrobel at feel good chiropractic, and Dr Bryan at live in ease chiropractic. Thank you, Heidi, for all of the care. Thank you for the honest talks, the celebrating the wins, encouraging my family, the dollhouse for my baby. Thank you for all of the support in and out of office. Thank you for helping me turn my pain into healing through gentle chiropractic care. Thank you, Bryan, for all of the time you give my husband and I. Thank you for always sharing your knowledge and giving us affordable prices so that we can continue care. Thank you for helping so much of our family and friends.

Thank you, Jennifer White, for the "overcoming overwhelm challenge." Thank you for the prizes you give, the time you give and the support you show. Thank you for cheering me on and inviting me to offer one of my books as a gift/prize during a challenge.

Thank you to anyone who has purchased any of my books. Anyone who comments or messages me about their reactions and experiences. To anyone who shared they are wanting to write their own book and came to me for support.

Thank you to my niece Syhara for sharing her love of dosisdeflores, skin care products. I am now into skin care and I actually enjoy the products. Mariana Flores is such a great soul; all good vibes and I am just so thankful to love the person as much as the products.

Thank you, Katie Hannus, for "the handmade." Through mothersquest I won a free consultation and products. I then signed up for the first two workshops she offered and I learned how to make elderberry syrup and fire cider. Everything kept falling into alignment. I am so thankful I was able to order ingredients from her and connect.

Thank you, Lindsay Pera, for "the mystics society." Thanks to scholarships and you offering opportunities as gifts/prizes for mothersquest challenges- I was able to participate in magic school and journey to right livelihood.

Thank you, Nicole Lee, for the scholarship space to be a part of "inclusive life, accelerator."

Thank you, Sheila, meeting you in person was just as amazing as meeting you virtually. Thank you for leading my daughter and I in workouts, journaling and reflecting on the beach. Thank you for "shift" (she is fit) free virtual meet ups for prayer, movement, and connection. Thank you for being more than a smiling face, more than thoughtful words. You even came through with flowers to celebrate my daughter and flowers for the both of us over holidays. I am so thankful I won a personalized gift package from you during the shift workout. Such beautiful artwork. Is there anything you don't do?

Thank you, Jeannette, for inviting me to be a guest on yours and Andrea Stevens "webs podcast." It was my first experience and you both made it so welcoming and so comfortable.

"I am celebrating that I was a guest on my first podcast. It's been a whole process of giving myself permission to take the time, to face fears and to step into something new. It has been a process of facing thoughts, re-framing and allowing the journey to be what it will be

who am I to be on a podcast? what will I say? am I good enough? am I successful enough? who am I to take up anyone's time?

anyways...it aired today...episode 46....

if anyone is curious, interested or bored and wants to listen.

this podcast I was asked to be on, is amazing (not because I am a guest on 1 episode)"

Thank you, author Natalie, my friend- for interviewing me. Not only that, but for always being there with insight when I have questions. Thank you for the calls and texts, being there to connect with. Thank you for the love, the support you give-for really seeing me- leaves me speechless constantly.

Thank you, to me. For finding the good through the struggle. For being thankful even in the struggle. Thank you for seeing this project through. Thank you for saying yes, to this and so much more. Thank you for putting your mental health first, I believe that has been what's gotten you through these pandemic times. Protecting our peace and caring for our mental health -is so important to me. Sometimes that means shifts will take place that you never would have wanted or thought would happen. But when you stick to your heart, life has a way of working out in the most beautiful and unexpected ways.

Thank you, mom and dad. Thank you for being my parents, for giving me life and for the ways you are involved in my life. I love and appreciate you both so much.

To anyone I did not mention. I did not forget you. I thank you all. You all mean so much to me, you know who you are.

What brings you happiness?

_____

_____

_____

_____

_____

_____

_____

_____

_____

_____

_____

A LITTLE ABOUT THE AUTHOR

Pandemic Poetry and reflections, is Author Carolina Ayala-Velasquez's second self-published book. Carolina, also known as Lena- has taken a break from teaching for the last three years. She has embraced inner healing and entrepreneurship. During this pandemic, she has embraced dreams from childhood and even new dreams. This book came as an idea just months before the year was ending, and now- it's real. She loves being a wife, mother, friend, daughter and author. She has dreams to write children's books, but is still learning what that path would look like and mean- to be polished and real and on shelfs in the stores.

Right now, she is enjoying taking each day- moment by moment. She is enjoying self-publishing her real, raw and unpolished poetry books that welcomes others into her life in this way.

A NOTE TO MY READERS

I know this may be a different type of book and reading. It is a mix of poetry, journal pages, Facebook posts and I do not have an editor. I know this book is in no particular order, dates are scattered, and groups are in no particular order of how events unfolded. Truth is, everything sometimes happened simultaneously. Everything is connected, whether the dates are "matched" up or not.

No-matter the "order" in which this came together, it doesn't matter. I hope dates, errors and diary pages don't scare you away.

I wrote this book for me. We had a day this year, when social media was down for hours. If social media was to ever be gone, so much of my life is there. I created this book so these stories, lessons and memories can exist beyond technology. I created this book because I wanted to self-publish another book before the year ended.

Maybe I rushed. Maybe I could have done more or different. Maybe, it is good enough, as is. I am going with that.

As of now, I have no idea what this book will look or feel like when it is actually printed and in my hands. It is scary to wonder, even as the writer.

Will it make sense? Will others relate? Will it be valuable?

Truth is, it's already done everything I hoped for. It was created. I did it! I am celebrating that.

This was a long process and it was challenging. I can't fit every journal, post or gold nugget. That just means, I will write more. The journey doesn't end here.

It is still, only the beginning.

If you take anything away, I hope you believe in yourself more. I hope you believe "if she can do it, I can do it."

Gratitude saved me, and I hope this book helps you to find gratitude in your daily life. I am thankful for you, whoever you are- however you ended up on any page of this book. Thank you. For your time and support.

www.ingramcontent.com/pod-product-compliance
Lightning Source LLC
Chambersburg PA
CBHW030347130626
46549CB00004B/1402